A Congo Chronicle
Patrice Lumumba in Urban Art

A Congo Chronicle
Patrice Lumumba in Urban Art

by
Bogumil Jewsiewicki
with contributions from
Dibwe dia Mwembu
Mary Nooter Roberts and Allen F. Roberts
Nyunda ya Rubango
Jean Omasombo Tshonda

Museum for African Art

A Congo Chronicle: Patrice Lumumba in Urban Art is published in
conjunction with an exhibition of the same title organized and presented
by the Museum for African Art, New York (23 April to 15 August 1999).
The exhibition will travel to other museums after its close in New York.

The exhibition is supported by grants from the Lannan Foundation,
the LEF Foundation, and Colgate-Palmolive Company.

Design: Alessia Ramaccia for Linda Florio Design

Library of Congress catalogue card number: 99-61072
Paperbound ISBN0-945802-25-0

Front cover: Lumumba, Master of the World.
By Burozi. ca. 1970s. Oil on cotton, 26 x 20 in.
Back cover: Lumumba breaking chains. By Burozi, signed Tshibumba, K.M.
Oil on fabric, 17 x 13 in.
Frontspiece: Fig. 1. *Lumumba en prison sous garde d'un militaire congolais*
[Lumumba in prison under guard of the Congolese military].
By Tinda Lwimba, ca. 1980s. Oil on cotton, 20¼ x 15 in.

Printed and bound in the U.S.A. by The Studley Press.
Photo credits: All catalogue objects by Frank Herreman.
Illustrations within essays as in caption credits.

Contents

Preface

It is with great excitement that the Museum for African Art presents **A Congo Chronicle: Patrice Lumumba in Urban Art**, an exhibition that will introduce many newcomers to the genre of Congolese Urban Art and the work of famed artist Tshibumba Kanda-Matulu. Tshibumba's work depicts the dramatic political career of Patrice Lumumba, the hero of Congo independence who became the nation's first Prime Minister in 1960, but was then killed after a few months in the midst of Cold War fervor. We invite visitors to experience the energy and intensity of the environment that gave birth to a cultural hero who became a symbol for the continuing transformation of Africa.

The twentieth century paintings in *A Congo Chronicle* share an underlying commonality with traditional African sculptural works—African art is purposeful. Whether the reason for its creation be spiritual or ritual as in the realm of traditional art, or for social change and societal communication as in the Urban Art featured in this exhibition, the works have intent beyond the aesthetic. African art is about many things; it is rarely, if ever, about art for art's sake.

It has been a fascinating experience to participate in the creation—and evolution—of this unusual exhibition which could not have materialized without the dedication and energy of many individuals.

First, our deep appreciation to our Guest Curator, renowned Africanist Bogumil Jewsiewicki of Quebec's Laval University, whose pioneering scholarship in the field of Urban Art has brought it to the attention of academics and art appreciators across continents.

We also gratefully acknowledge the dedicated professionals at the Museum for African Art, each of whom has made an invaluable contribution to this exhibition and catalogue. Frank Herreman, Director of Exhibitions and Mark D'Amato, Associate Curator who worked closely with our Guest Curator to create this original exhibition; Carol Braide, Curatorial Assistant/Publication Coordinator, for her assistance with the exhibition and the publication of this catalogue; Lubangi Muniania of the Education Department and Andrei Nadler in Finance. Thank you one and all for your hard work and commitment to excellence.

Finally, we thank the Lannan Foundation and the LEF Foundation for their support which enables the Museum to fulfill its mission of sharing the glories of African art and culture.

Elsie Crum McCabe   Anne H. Stark
President   *Deputy Director*

March 1999

Acknowledgments

Bogumil Jewsiewicki

This catalogue and exhibition are the result of a long process in which my understanding of the forms and materials used by ordinary Congolese people to master their future in imagination was developed and deepened through exchanges with both colleagues in the academy and popular producers of social knowledge. I am pleased to share the space of this catalogue with three such colleagues. I would also like to express my gratitude to all those persons who for the last thirty years have guided me in a dialogue with the knowledge that the Congolese construct about themselves and the world. These are first and foremost the painters, too numerous to name here; also the musicians; and all the men and women who have allowed me to be present and to participate in their conversations about knowledge and beauty.

It is impossible to thank all the researchers who worked with me by name. Let me cite the leaders of the research team: Biaya T. K., Dibwe dia Mwembu, and Nzunguba Ibio. I am also profoundly grateful to Victor Bol, Johannes Fabian, Ilona Szombati, Léon Verbeek, and Edouard Vincke for making both their collections and their knowledge of Congolese paintings and painters available to me. My research in the Congo would not have been possible without the assistance of Jeffrey J. Hoover and Léon Verbeek. I received several research grants from the Social Science Research Council of Canada. The Canada Council, the Woodrow Wilson Center for International Scholars, the Forschungszentrum Kulturwissenschaften in Vienna, and the Ecole des Hautes Etudes en Sciences Sociales in Paris also enabled me to develop my thinking on this subject. The Centre d'Etudes Africaines at the Ecole des Hautes Etudes, the CELAT (Centre d'études interdisciplinaires sur les lettres, les arts et les traditions) of the Université Laval, and the Amrad Gallery in Montreal respectively made possible the publication of a special issue of *Cahiers d'Etudes Africaines*, on images; of a collective work on Tshibumba Kanda Matulu entitled *Art pictural zaïrois*; and of a book on the Zairean painter Chéri Samba entitled *Hybridity of an Art*. These were crucial stages in my work on painting in Africa.

It is certainly no coincidence that this exhibition has been realized with the Museum for African Art. My collaboration with the Museum goes back to the "Africa Explores" exhibition of 1991. I owe a great deal to conversations with Susan Vogel, then the Museum director, and later with Polly Nooter Roberts, both of whom share and support my conviction that the shock of colonial occupation did not stop African men and women from either producing or consuming art; rather their ways of making art underwent different transformations from Western art. In its first conception, the exhibition was planned to accompany "Memory: Luba Art and the Making of History," at the Museum in 1996. That conception could not be realized, but the dialogue was never broken off, as is attested to by Polly Nooter Roberts and Allen Roberts's essay in this catalogue.

The reader owes much to Amy Jacobs, who artfully translated many of these essays from French into English, and to David Frankel and Elizabeth Franzen, who polished the English translations.

Finally, I could never have conceived this exhibition or catalogue without the hospitality and friendship of a great many Congolese who were willing to instruct an ignorant foreigner in their culture. For this to take place, I had first to go to and be in their country; for this I thank Hala and Dzidek Zakrzewscy. And to receive that instruction, my own cultural perspective needed opening up; this I owe to Gustaaf Hulstaert and Jan Vansina. I dedicate this work to them.

Lenders to the Exhibition

James Bullard
Victor Bol
Bogumil Jewsiewicki
Léon Verbeek
Eduoard Vincke

Contributors

Individual

Mr. & Mrs. Armand P. Arman
Mr. & Mrs. Charles B. Benenson
Bernice & Sidney Clyman
Jane & Gerald Katcher
Drs. Marian & Daniel Malcolm
Ms. Kathryn McAuliffe
Mr. Don H. Nelson
Mr. & Mrs. James J. Ross
Lynne & Robert Rubin
Daniel Shapiro & Agnes Gund
Cecilia & Irwin Smiley
Mr. Jason H. Wright

Mr. & Mrs. Richard Faletti
M.J. & Caral G. Lebworth
Jerome & Ellen Stern
Mr. & Mrs. Victor Teicher

Mr. & Mrs. Lewis B. Cullman
Mr. Irwin Ginsburg
Denyse & Marc Ginzberg
Mr. Lawrence Gussman
Mr. & Mrs. Sol Levitt
Mr. Rodney M. Miller
Mr. Richard Solomon & Ms. Lisa Bradley
Dr. & Mrs. Bernard M. Wagner
Harold & Maureen Zarember

Mr. S. Thomas Alexander, III
Mr. & Mrs. Carroll Cline
Kurt & Mary Delbanco
Mr. Lance Entwistle
Ms. Roberta Entwistle
Ms. Meredith Finch
Dr. Suzanne Frye
Mr. & Mrs. Jacques Germain
Mr. & Mrs. Stephen Humanitzki
Diane & Brian Leyden
Dr. & Mrs. Andreas Linder
Mr. Leonard Milberg
Ms. Denise Murrell
Mr. Michael Oliver
Mr. & Mrs. Marvin Ross-Greifinger
Mrs. Harry Rubin
Mr. Merton D. Simpson
Mr. & Mrs. Saul Stanoff

Mr. Richard White
Mr. Daniel M. Ziff

Mr. & Mrs. Arnold Alderman
Robert R. Banks
Walter & Molly Bareiss
Arthur & Phyllis Bargonetti
Ms. Joan Barist
Dr. & Mrs. Samuel Berkowitz
Owen & Mary Blicksilver
Dr. Jean Borgatti Ernest P. Bynum
  & Dennis M.Costin
Mr. Jeffrey Cohen
Ms. Ann Coiro
Lisa & Gerald Dannenberg
Dr. D. David Dershaw
Ms. Nancy D. Field
Ms. Vianna Finch
Dr. & Mrs. Gilbert Graham
Ms. Barbara Hoffman
Mr. David Holbrook
Mr. & Mrs. Bernard Jaffe
Mr. Lloyd Sheldon Johnson
Mr. Luciano Lanfranchi
Mr. & Mrs. Guy Lanquetot
Mr. & Mrs. Samuel Lurie
Mrs. Kendall A. Mix
Donald & Florence Morris
Dr. Werner Muensterberger
Mr. Peter Mullett &
Ms. Heather Heinlein
Ms. Sylvia Owen &
Dr. Bernard Fabricius
Mr. John Pantazis
Ms. Sandra Packer Pine
Mr. & Mrs. Fred M. Richman
Ms. Beatrice Riese
Holly & David Ross
Mr. & Mrs. Arthur Sarnoff
Mr. Sydney L. Shaper
Ms. Mary Jo Shepard
Cherie & Edwin Silver
Mr. & Mrs. Kenneth Snelson
Mr. Howard Tanenbaum
Mr. Lucien Van de Velde
Ms. Kathy van der Pas
Dr. & Mrs. Leon Wallace
Mr. Willet Weeks
George & Joyce Wein
Michelle & Claude Winfield
Mr. John F. Zulack

Corporate & Institutional

The Buhl Foundation, Inc.
The Chase Manhattan Corporation
The Irene Diamond Fund
The Max and Victoria Dreyfus Foundation
Metropolitan Life Foundation
RJR Nabisco Foundation
Zeneca Pharmaceuticals
ABC, Inc.
Arnold Industries
Arthur Andersen & Co.
Bayer Corporation
Bell Atlantic Foundation
The Coca-Cola Company
Consolidated Edison Company of
  New York, Inc.
Davis, Scott, Weber & Edwards P.C.
Davis Polk & Wardwell
De Coziart Perpetual Trust
Donaldson Lufkin & Jenrette Securities
  Corporation
Entrust Capital, Inc.
The Equitable Foundation
Evercore Partners, Inc.
Fund for the City of New York
IBM
J.P. Morgan Charitable Trust
William H. Kearns Foundation
Lannan Foundation
The LEF Foundation
Merrill Lynch & Co.
New York Life Insurance Company
Oceanie-Afrique Noire
Pace Editions, Inc.
The Peninsula Foundation
PepsiCo., Inc.
Pfizer
S & B Capital
Salomon Smith Barney
Texaco, Inc.
Time Warner Inc.
Henry van Ameringen Foundation
VOLVO
Xerox Foundation

American Express
Arthur Ashe, Inc.
Bloomberg News
Bloomcraft
BSMG Worldwide
Comix, Inc.
Charles E. Culpeper Foundation
DC 37 Local 1549 NYC Clerical
Deloitte & Touche LLP
Dime Savings Bank

Introduction

Bogumil Jewsiewicki

In the 1960s, vast numbers of Africans acquired independence from the colonial powers. Now, in the 1990s, in Congo and throughout Africa (not to mention the rest of the world), living testimony of the events of that decade is giving way to memory and history. Historians and other cultural brokers have taken charge of knowledge of the period, which between the Second World War and the relatively peaceful demise of the Soviet system, profoundly changed the second half of the twentieth century. As eyewitnesses of the events of the 1960s grow old and die, social knowledge becomes detached from experience, surviving only through the links that may be constructed, either by art or by academic knowledge, between the things that happened then (of which there remains only anever fainter trace) and the social demand to understand them in relation to what's happening now—the past as we reconstruct it in the present.

For the last twenty years, the West—and particularly North America—has been trumpeting the end of the big metanarratives, their inability to account for present experience and give meaning to the past. There is a serious risk that this part of the world will confuse its own story with the future of all humanity, as it has for the last two hundred years. Meanwhile arious national, regional, and in some cases ethnic narratives, including pictorial and performative narrative forms, are reconfiguring the past, shaping knowledge to make it consistent with an affirmation of political identity.

The majority of humanity claims the right to imagine and formulate a collective identity in political and narrative terms—narration is a crucial political instrument. In the West, narrative has played a particular in, for example, novel, and before that in Christianity, the religion that the West has made its own. This is a historical fact, but it in no way allows us to claim that when other societies narrate, they are recycling a Western tool. Those societies make their own tools, and a great variety of them—tools that are both adapted to local conditions and remain understandable from one region of the world to another, like a pop song or an Indian movie that cannot be owned by the West.

It is in this perspective that the question of what is known of Patrice Lumumba, founding hero of a new political order in Congo, in Africa, and we may even say among all the "oppressed of the earth," is explored here. The 1990s have seen the figure of Lumumba replaced by that of Nelson Mandela, yet Lumumba the romantic hero, symbol of a painful coming-to-be through revolution, cannot really be opposed to Mandela, the wise man moving forward to full dignity by means of pardon and negotiation.

Lumumba is rather the other side of Mandela. And the essays collected here propose, each in its own way, a reading of narrative constructions of Lumumba, particularly visual narratives. The Lumumba imagined, the Lumumba represented, is a figure who speaks and makes the viewer speak, but he does not tell his own story, and his story is only rarely told. It is rather in relation to Lumumba as the present has constructed him that social actors recount their experiences and formulate their conception of a just political order. Lumumba is a realm of memory where men and women make use of their knowledge of the past and their experience of the present, and on the basis of which they demand recognition of their dignity.

In proposing to the reader who visits this exhibition an experience of Lumumba as a realm of Congolese memory, a realm on the basis of which the Congolese affirm their right to dignity and their aptness to speak in the name of all humanity, it is important to clarify one thing. The norms of social communication, the narrative conventions, and the aesthetic canons operative in the urban societies of Congo are not the same as those of North America. Steering clear of loco-centrism, we should not assume that because Congolese painters use the same tools as Western painters, they are trying to obtain the same effects. To give just one example, repetition, about which Western culture is ambivalent, is a valued stylistic trope in Congo, while radical innovation has little role in Congolese communication, which is structured by an aesthetics of reception. We cannot annex Congolese painting to the history of Western painting. Let us try instead to participate actively in the dialogue between the paintings and the documents that the painters have used as local memory; between the paintings and the essays, especially those written by Congolese researchers; and lastly between Lumumba as painted and Lumumba as represented in books, narratives, and songs. The political space of the years 1960 to 1980—a space, it must be admitted, that like the working men's bar was exclusively male—was a place of political debate. Let us go, men and women, into that spaceand participate in that debate.

Let the reader and visitor also be aware of a radical change that has not been our primary focus here. During most of the second half of the twentieth century, politics as a sphere of knowledge and action was a male domain, for historical reasons concerning access to modernity through salaried work, which in the Belgian Congo only men could have. Today, however, in the last decade of the twentieth century, such knowledge is constructed and debated not in working men's bars but in churches and social associations. Family survival is no longer guaranteed by the salary of working men but by the resourcefulness and street-smarts of women and children. And the political space is no longer the bar but the house of prayer or the marketplace.

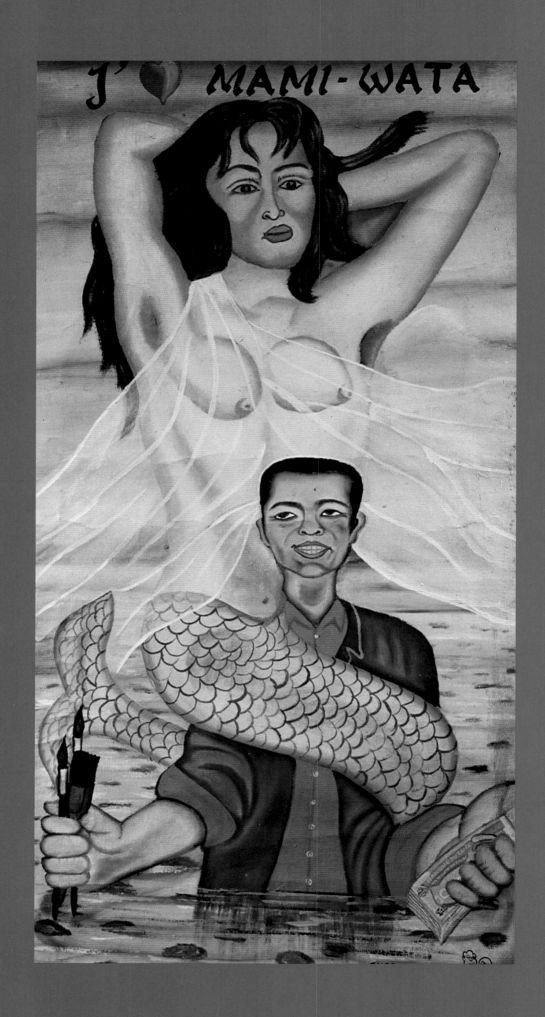

Popular Painting in Contemporary Katanga: Painters, Audiences, Buyers, and Sociopolitical Contexts

Bogumil Jewsiewicki

No Lubumbashi popular painter has had an international career like that of the Kinshasa artist Chéri Samba; and there are in fact a number of artists and musicians in Kinshasa whom the whirlwind of international success has whisked farther from local audiences than any artist in Lubumbashi, and not only in Lubumbashi but in the surrounding province of Katanga (Jewsiewicki 1995). These are just two of many differences between the societies and cultures of these two cities, a difference that has held true in both the colonial and the postcolonial periods. Since the 1920s, Kinshasa has thrived as the seat of the country's political power and the primary center of its commercial and administrative activities. Lubumbashi, on the other hand, is a town of hard labor and laborers. In the Congolese social imagination, Kinshasa—"Kin la Belle"—is where one risks all to gain all, where success and failure are decided in a single stroke. In Lubumbashi, the primary values are perseverance and continuity.

Even the respective languages of Kinshasa and Lubumbashi, both of them chosen by the colonizers to satisfy the different objectives they had set for the two cities, are adapted to these different demands. Kinshasans speak Lingala, the language of administration and commerce, and formerly also the language of the colonial army. Under General Joseph-Désiré Mobutu, Lingala was the unofficial state language, and it is also the language of popular song (Fabian 1989). Meanwhile Kingwana, the version of Swahili spoken in Lubumbashi, is the language of industrial labor (ibid.). Both languages were once used to communicate between masters and workers, to transmit orders and secure obedience. Later, though, each became a tool in creating a distinct urban culture.

Kinshasa is the city of excesses and extremes, a place where men pass like comets, making their mark immediately or not at all. In Lubumbashi, though, especially in the workers' camps of the Union minière du Haut Katanga (Mining Union of Upper Katanga), the team is valued over the individual, the long-term over the moment. In the social and cultural life of Kinshasa, independence has meant replacing white authority with African authority; in Lubumbashi the managerial and technological authority of Westerners has remained in place, despite sometimes violent attempts to end it. Kinshasa has always thought of itself as competing with Brazzaville, its sister city across the river in the neighboring Republic of Congo, while Lubumbashi is just one stopping-off point in the technologically, culturally, humanly continuous expanse of southern Africa. Even before independence, Kinshasa was growing at a mad pace, swelling with new arrivals drawn to the mirage of success; meanwhile the population of Lubumbashi has fluctuated with the demand for industrial

Fig. 2.
I Love Mami-Wata. By Chéri-Benga, 1993. Oil on fabric. 35 1/8 x 16 1/2 in.

FIG. 3.
Temps arabe, 1789. [Arab Time, 1789].
By Angali, 1984. Oil on fabric, 17 x 30½ in.
Slave caravan.

FIG. 4.
Colonie belge, 1909-1959. [Belgian Colony,
1909-1959]. By Nkulu wa Nkulu. Oil on fabric,
15½ x 21¾ in. Prisoners chained as were the
slaves in Arab time.

labor. Few Lubumbashi artists have ever acquired international renown, and those who have—among them Pilipili and Mwenze, who may be classified as naive artists, and the virtuoso guitarist Jean-Bosco Mwenda—are unknown outside a small circle of connoisseurs.

The cultures of these two urban centers, including the types of popular painting done in them, do share common features, including what I call the primary icons: the mermaid (*mami wata*) (fig. 2); the Belgian colony (fig. 4); the forced march of the slaves (fig. 3); even *inakale* (fig. 5), the man caught between three mortal dangers (snake, crocodile, and lion or leopard). They differ, however, in style—the formal means of communicating with the viewer—and in the presence of implicit references to local history, of which there are many in Lubumbashi painting and almost none in Kinshasan. The visual language of Kinshasa is spectacular: bright colors, explosive renderings, esthetic and moral daring— nudity (fig. 2), for example. Lubumbashi painting is more concerned with dialogue, appealing both to the public's shared memories of the city's history and to the distinct strands of memory of the major ethnic groups, and constructing a sense of continuous belonging to the city's urban culture, especially for the industrial workers there. Lubumbashi painting is addressed less to the individual than to the group, among which it catalyzes conversation. In this kind of social production of meaning, painting functions like, and together with, urban theater (for example that of Mufwankolo, organizer and leader of a series of theater troupes, who has been composing and staging plays on local life for over thirty years; see Fabian 1990) and music (namely that of Baba Gaston and Jean-Bosco Mwenda, two Katangese songwriters and singers who were very popular in the 1960s). Whereas Kinshasans may brazenly call attention to themselves, in Lubumbashi such behavior is considered indecent, even obscene. (It is true that Lubumbashi artists may produce pornographic paintings, but these are meant to be shown only in hotels used by prostitutes, and are perceived as visual "how to" instructions rather than erotic stimulants.)

The work of the Kinshasan Chéri Samba, a postmodern artist of international renown, is exuberant and provocative. When the Lubumbashi artist Tshibumba Kanda was active, by contrast, he was known for application, perseverance, and will to instruct. A similar comparison could be made between Moke, from Kinshasa, and Burozi, from Lubumbashi. Like Samba and Moke, Tshibumba met Westerners who wanted to help him, and who might have propelled him to an international career. It is true that Johannes Fabian and myself, as well as a handful of other researcher-professors, did not perhaps promote him in the same way that Pierre Haffner promoted Moke, or Didier de Lannoy promoted Chéri Samba; I should also mention Jean-Marc Patras, who was extremely helpful to both of these Kinshasa artists. Still, Gilles Moal, the last Westerner for whom Tshibumba worked—he signed a contract to sell Moal all his paintings—could have played a role comparable to that of Haffner and de Lannoy. And the fact that he did not successfully establish Tshibumba's art may be in part explained by the different urban cultures of the two cities, and by the different local perceptions of the social role of the painter. There is also a profound difference in the preaching style and intentions of painter-preachers: Frère Bodo of Kinshasa terrorizes sinners with the specter of the Last Judgment, while Burozi of Lubumbashi tries to convince them of divine mercy, so that they may come to feel remorse.

The Ethics and Esthetics of a Particular Social Experience of the World

Present-day popular painting began to develop in industrial Katanga when the Frenchman Pierre Romain-Desfossés became taken with the spontaneous creativity of a few young local men (Cornelis 1998). Romain-Desfossés was a painter who settled in Lubumbashi in the mid-1940s. For him, African urban art could only be decorative in character and could only take its inspiration from ethnic folklore, and his advice to these first painters had the effect of confining them to his particular aesthetic. The young artists produced paintings for an art market of Western amateurs of naive art, and later, very briefly, for the political and economic institutions of Katanga when it was temporarily independent, in 1960–63. Subsequently, since under Mobutu's dictatorship anything that could be interpreted as evoking a distinct regional Katangese identity was forbidden, these artists remained on the margins of the national art scene for thirty years.

In the last years of the colony, with the help of Laurent Moonens, a Belgian artist first active in Kinshasa in the 1940s, the Académie des Beaux-Arts de Lubumbashi began training African students in the applied and decorative arts (Toebosch 1992). At the end of the 1950s, art competitions and exhibitions were organized in the city around the theme "Making Good Citizens." There was, for example, a competition to show art demonstrating the benefits of electricity.

FIG. 5.
Inakale [No way out]. By M.Maka, 1996. Oil on fabric, 19½ x 24 in.

The contrast between Lubumbashi and Kinshasa is striking. In Kinshasa, too, urban painting was launched and helped along by two Westerners: Maurice Alhadeff, a businessman from the island of Rhodes, and Victor Wallenda, a Belgian missionary. Alhadeff—himself the city's primary patron of popular art—was also concerned to get the artwork into the local and international marketplace. (In this he resembled the merchants of Greek origin who created the local market for urban music.) Wallenda for his part founded the Kinshasa Académie des Beaux Arts, which in its first decade of existence was respectful of Congolese art-making traditions. It later offered training in Western-style art, and students were made aware of the Western notion of the artist's vocation (see Cornet, de Cnodder, Diericks, and Toebosch 1989).

Painting for a local urban public also developed in both Kinshasa and Lubumbashi, although only on the margins of an artistic production that was primarily aimed at foreigners temporarily settled in Congo, and that sometimes—with luck—reached the institutions of the modern state and economy. Such painting was given very little place in local museums; a few purchases were made in the mid-1970s, but did not develop into an acquisitions practice. There were only a handful of private collections. No critical attention has ever been paid to popular painting (with the exception of the work of Badi-Banga ne-Mwine from Kinshasa), which makes it hard to give a systematic account of the art's development, particularly in Katanga. The following presentation is based primarily on my own art collection; on the collections of Johannes Fabian and Ilona Szombati, Victor Bol, Edouard Vincke, and Léon Verbeek; and on continued research and contact with painters and their viewers. Because in Congo a popular painting is as much a social discourse as an esthetic experience, I have adopted a sociocritical approach, according to which we may first of all distinguish three main pictorial genres.

Of Modernity, the Individual, and Resemblance

Mechanically reproduced images—that is, photographs and printed religious images—are widely circulated in Congo, and in the cities they are the principle source for creating other forms of visual communication. Photography in the region is more than an aid to memory; it plays a crucial role in constructing the modern person. Here I am referring above all to men, specifically those Congolese men who became actors first in economic life—salaried workers—and later in political life. Until the late 1940s, an individual worker stayed only a limited time in the city before going back to the village. He used photography to construct a memory of himself as a modern, elegant man, a man who had succeeded in the colonial universe. At the same time, photography also made it possible for him to assimilate himself to a traditional cultural hero. Such heroes had long been shown with objects and signs associated with them, objects that they were in some cases understood to have invented (Nooter Roberts 1996) or at least to have introduced to the community. A salaried worker followed the same hero-making process by having himself photographed with objects that characterized his modern work activity, or with which, at any rate, he wanted to be associated.

In this cultural world, mimetic representation of the individual person matters little. Memory works instead from name and attribute. To have one's photograph taken next to a bicycle or a sewing machine, or wearing glasses that one doesn't really need, partakes of the same kind of self-heroicizing involved in giving oneself the name "Kapitula" ("shorts," at one time the distinctive dress of Africans working for whites), "Belegi" (Belgian), or "Usungu" (from *muzungu,* white). Photography becomes a realm in which the individual is remembered. Mechanically produced and acquired as merchandise, the photograph inscribes the identity of its subject first in the colonial world, then in the modern world, where having a salary—and, later, participating in political activity—means having money, and thereby gaining access to consumer goods, access that villagers didn't have.

At the beginning of the 1970s, the state required each individual to carry a photo identity card. This document replaced the real person with "the citizen," a subject of the state. Of course people immediately began falsifying the cards, taking on new identities as needed— identities that would get them access to a given service, allow them to pass an inspection, and so forth. Nevertheless, it was the identity card—and especially its photograph—more than one's flesh-and-blood substance that constituted one's official identity. And this led to a generalized understanding that, in modernity, the subject of the state was constructed out of mimetic and mechanical images. Because photographs represent this experience of being inscribed within the state, portraits in Congo are painted from them, and identity-card photos are the preferred model. Doubly "true," such portraits present a modern self—the objects in the painting attest to that modernity—while also evoking the mechanical image (the photograph) and thus the sitter's "political" identity (fig. 6).

Fig. 6.
Portrail of a man. By unknown artist.
Oil on fabric, 18¹/₂ x 16¹/₂ in.

Images of saints, distributed mainly to children in Catholic schools (the Christian missions long had a monopoly on teaching, and the best schools continue to be Christian ones), reinforce the perception that mechanically reproduced images are a Christian and therefore modern form of presence. No doubt the missionaries had to work to keep people from adoring the image instead of the saint; nevertheless, it was by means of the image that the saint was understood to protect, guide, serve as a model—in sum, to be present. The mechanically reproduced image was the earthly reality of a saint whom one could not know in person, and with whom, in contrast to an ancestor, one had no social relation. One shared no memory with the saint, only a book: the written narrative of his or her life.

This is crucial to understanding the conventions governing the execution and interpretation of popular paintings. To paint someone's portrait is to situate that person in modernity. Memory does not try to keep a person's facial features recognizable, in the sense of mimetic representation, but rather places that person in the ordinary—from colonial times on the (questionable) term used has been "customary"—universe of social relations. It is not that there is no attempt to identify the person, but that identification is effected above all through certain attributes (Nooter Roberts 1996, Roberts 1996), and through the affirmation of social and familial ties, that is, through genealogy. In the colonial universe and later in the modern one, mimetic identification—first the photo I.D., then the painted portrait—constitutes a discourse on modernity and the place one occupies in it.

In the Congolese context, a discourse on modernity is a discourse on power—especially political power—and on the cost of having a share of it. For this reason, but also with the intention of individualizing the female mermaid's face, the mami wata icon belongs to this same pictorial genre. There is no generic *mami wata;* she is not a goddess. Rather, any brave man with a stroke of luck can have his personal *mami wata.* In Congo this discourse is essentially visual: there is relatively little oral narrative on the *mami wata,* but there are countless paintings. These images constitute a discourse on the seductive power of modernity, to which one accedes, by paying a price, through a female figure. The fact that seduction, and also abduction, are used as metaphors for the historical experience of salaried men (particularly manual laborers but also low-level office workers) reflects two characteristics of the urban universe. First, it long remained a world of men, who had to compete for the few women present. Second, those women could not become legitimate wives and mothers, and therefore could not provide a man access to the future status of ancestor. Because they often had no parents living in the city who could provide a dowry (considered a proof of a child's legitimacy), they were mere simulacra. Like money, *they* seemed to decide the conditions under which men might possess them (fig. 2). They were as arbitrary and unpredictable as luck—or as modern political power.

FIG. 7.
Colonie 1959 [Colony 1959]. Unsigned.
Oil on fabric, 16½ x 22¾ in.

FIG. 8.
Colonie belge, 1885 - 1959 [Belgian Colony
1885-1959]. By Tshibumba.
Oil on fabric, 13¾ x 20⅞ in.

Just as luck and the free woman comprised the main subject of urban music, especially in the late 1950s and early '60s, so *mami wata* became the main subject of painting in the 1970s. This icon of urban Congolese memory—a full-fledged realm of memory—is associated regionally with numerous beliefs in water spirits. There are resonances in it of nineteenth-century West African narratives on the cult of *mami wata* (the term actually derives from the English words "Mummy Water"), and in Congolese memory of the colonial white woman, considered an idle creature, attribute of the white man's power, and strictly forbidden to blacks. Here we may cite an anecdote from the Lubumbashi archives: in the 1950s a Belgian woman married to a Congolese man came to live with her husband in Elisabethville (Lubumbashi). This situation had never before been encountered in the colony, and after searching long and hard for a solution to the question of where the couple would live, the provincial administration decided to settle them in the white quarter. The black man was made to transgress the racial barrier because it was unthinkable for a white woman to live among blacks.

In Lubumbashi the mermaid is called *mamba muntu*, probably in reference to the snake that always accompanies her. (The first meaning of *mamba* is crocodile, but in Lubumbashi it also means snake, which can be understood as the Christian symbol of Satanic temptation.) In both Lubumbashi and Kinshasa the main clients for paintings of her have been civil servants, army officers, and the petty bourgeoisie—under Mobutu, a highly mobile social category. Closely linked to the state, these constituencies adopted Lingala as their language of communication and were active in the cultural uniformization of the nation. The whole country was convinced that Mobutu drew his political strength from his personal *mami wata,* and that one of the first official holidays he decreed—the feast day of the fish—was actually dedicated to her.

Memory and Pictorial Narration of History

Another genre of popular painting uses memory of the past to create a discourse on the present. The same icons appear in this genre throughout the nation, but there are significant regional differences in execution. This is visual memory in a proper use of the term, involving the convening of common recollections charged with social meaning. It is therefore highly powerful.

The national icon par excellence (figs. 7, 8) is "The Belgian colony" (also called "The whip," especially in the eastern part of the country). This icon is executed differently from city to city and from region to region; it is an example of a realm in which national memory of the colonial period encounters regional memory in its various strands. Personal and family recollections are manifest in this first image of common memory. The painter asks where his client is originally from, then inscribes the name of the corresponding territory on the administrative building that more often than not is positioned in the painting's center background. In this way national memory is "personalized." Under cover of the colonial past, the "Belgian colony" icon deals with relations between the state and its subjects, between power and those over whom power is exercised. It clearly indicates that the dominant form of the political tie is violence; and it shows that the political field is reserved for men. Men exercise power, and submit to it; when women are in the picture, they are only there to express the people's suffering.

Fig. 9.
La guerre de 80 jours [The 80 Day War].
By Abis, 1996. Oil on fabric, 20 x 27¼ in.

Lubumbashi painting includes several other historical icons, regional realms of memory referring above all to national independence as experienced locally in Katanga's attempt to secede from the new nation. This memory is specifically Katangese; it stands in opposition to the memory of the nation. Two icons preserve realms of memory from precolonial times: the forced march of the slaves, a national icon, and Ngongo Leteta, a regional figure of the nineteenth century (see my article in the present volume on memory of Lumumba).

Understanding the Present: Painted Images and Rumor

The third pictorial genre may be described as a chronicle of the present, a kind of visual representation of the man-in-the-street's idea of current events. The epistemology of rumor, at least in Congo, involves the idea that information that has been repeated by several tongues, has traversed one or more social networks, and in doing so has passed the test of being interesting or relevant. Whether it is factually true or not doesn't matter; it is important in either case. The same is true for declaring one's identity within a social group: what counts socially is what people are willing to accept as true under certain conditions—what they agree to accredit even though they know it is factually inaccurate. This genre includes scenes of villages in the middle of a forest, next to flowing streams (fig. 10), and so forth. Displayed in an urban home, such a painting should not be seen as a generic landscape; instead it shows that the master of the house has his social origins in the village figured. (This means that a male ancestor was born there, from whom the individual in question has acquired rights of membership.) His identity is thus legitimately inscribed in tradition ("custom"); he has his place in a precolonial political space, and by virtue of this is understood to be a citizen of the modern state.

In this genre the painters represent many contemporary events, generally in a very schematic way, without any attempt to give mimetic resemblance to places or persons. Individual or group memory conserves knowledge of the event in question; it has become social knowledge. There is therefore no need—indeed it would be redundant—to make a visually explicit identification. A text written into the image, or added like a caption beneath it, may call attention to contested points of a "historical" fact, recalling that here memory and history—especially official history—are in disaccord. These paintings present, in social, public space, all that deserves to be debated or should be kept alive and present in people's minds. They propose present-day realms of memory, many of which will not survive the test of social experience. What we have here is a kind of icon library in which images come and go without their individual futures in collective memory being predictable. The painting is a realm of present-day memory, not a testament to the veracity of the event, place, or person to whom it refers; the authenticity of any such testament would have to be proven. To those who have not experienced this realm, or who want an account of it, the painting proposes a kind of "virtual" experience, and thereby makes it possible to verify the particular memory's relevance for the present (figs. 9, 12). The historical fact, once it has happened, is merely a referent. It has its importance, of course, given that it localizes memory in political and social space; but memory does its work from the icon, not from the fact.

Fig. 10.
Village scene. By Dekab, 1968.
Oil on fabric, 17¼ x 21¾ in.

Fig. 11.
Kabila chasing out Mobutu. By Production Congo, 1997. Oil on fabric, 18¼ x 24½ in.

The Popular Painter: Wise Man or Expert?

Being a Painter in Katanga

Who are these popular painters, and how do they practice their craft? A quick though insufficient answer is that they are self-employed workers making their living within the unofficial economy. Most of them say they would be willing to combine this livelihood with another, or to abandon it for another if they could no longer support themselves with it. In both their self-perception and the understanding of their audience, painting is a craft, not a vocation; to abandon it would imply not self-betrayal but simply adapting in order to survive. Several painters have quit, including Tshibumba himself. And those who keep at it despite the enormous reduction in their clientele during the economic crisis probably do so because things are just as bad elsewhere: everyone is trying to sell something, but almost no one is buying (except, of course, for staple foods).

Fig. 12.
Lumumbashi, une nouvelle Chicago - Coup du 31 Mars 1980. [Lumumbashi, the new Chicago, holdup of 31 March 1980]. By Tshibumba, K.M. Oil on fabric, 13½ x 20¼ in.

There is also the fact that being a painter requires an initial financial investment. This investment is not very large, but once the money is spent, it is not in the painter's interest to quit. First, when better economic times arrive, it will be harder for him to set himself up again than to continue a going business, even a marginal one. Also, to be a painter one needs paint, a few brushes, some fabric. Costs can be kept very low: some painters make their own brushes, and use pieces of old cloth—shirttails, a bit of sheet—for canvas. Colors must be bought, but if a painter is broke he may paint only in black, concocted from soot or a bit of burnt tire (fig. 11). Paintings in black and white, however, sell for less, if they sell at all; and painters working in black have no opportunity to sell advertising (fig. 15) or religious images, which people always want in color. Once a painter is reduced to black, only a commission from someone who has access to an external market and is willing to give him an advance can really enable him to paint again.

Painters who have attended the local art school think of themselves as belonging to another category altogether, and others tacitly agree. Some claim to be artists in the Western sense. As long as they could make a living from the tourist market and from foreign collectors of naive art, these artists did not do popular painting, but followed the techniques they had learned at school, using real art materials and painting at an easel (figs. 16–18).

Fig. 13.
Back of painting, fig. 15. Printed cotton. 24 x 19 in.

The popular painters certainly envy the relative material well-being available to some of the trained artists, but they have no way of selling to foreigners, except for very occasional works commissioned by foreign dealers (generally of Mediterranean origin, and generally only interested in painted reproductions of paintings by Western artists) and by missionaries. A first breach in the wall separating these two types of painters occurred in the 1970s, when a few Westerners "discovered" popular painting and included it in the first exhibition of Congolese work as *national* art. The exhibition, entitled "Sura Dja" (Faces and Roots of Zaire), was held at the Musée des arts décoratifs, Paris, in 1982. It included not only painters from the Romain-Desfossés school but "popular" painters, some of whom later got prices for their work comparable to those paid for naive painting.

In the mid-1980s, foreigners began leaving Congo in droves, forcing several academy-trained painters to look for work in the local, indigenous market. Some of them even got themselves hired as apprentices to popular painters in order to familiarize themselves

FIG. 14.
Back of painting (mirror image).
Flour sack, 32 x 22 in.

with this market's themes and aesthetic conventions. All have chosen to paint on canvases made of flour sacking—*the* material used by popular painters—or, when that cannot be had, on whatever fabric can (figs 13, 14). Oil paints in tubes have been replaced by house paints. A canvas can consist of a piece of fabric pulled onto a frame made of four sticks, then leaned against the back of a chair set in the shade—for the painter's studio is either the common space of a shared housing lot or the public space of the street. Except for those done as advertising or as decorations in bars, the paintings are small, both because people's houses are small and low, and because using more material would push up the selling price, and the painting has to be cheap to find a buyer. All purchases involve vigorous bargaining. Still, in Mbujimayi, the country's diamond capital, prices have remained high: paintings can sell for as high as $300 there, compared to $30 in Lubumbashi. At those prices the painters in Mbujimayi can work on easels and in oil.

Who "Authors" a Painting?

In 1996 the popular painter Matanda wa Matanda, who had resigned himself to working as a night-watchman, received a commission from a collaborator of mine who introduced himself as a dealer. The commission—for 20 canvases, on whatever subjects inspired him—was only partly executed by Matanda, who no longer had any equipment and was in dire need of money. So he ceded part of the commission to another painter, Abis, who regularly produced advertising signs for local merchants, so that he was still able to work in color while Matanda was confined to black and white. All of the paintings were signed "Matanda," however, and it was Matanda who delivered them to the buyer.

This example—one of many in my personal experience—points up the major difference beween the conception of the artist in the West and in Congo. In Congo the painter is a worker, and his real challenge is not to produce but to sell. A painting's "author" is therefore the man who is directly in communication with the client, with whom he discusses both the content and the price of the commission. A sale is proof that the product has met a need, and therefore of the product's and its producer's relevance. In this context the notion of the author and of intellectual property comes to mean that crucial juncture where a product meets proof of its relevance.

FIG. 15.
Salon de Coiffure [Hairstyling Salon].
By Abis, 1996. Oil on fabric, 24 x 19 in.

Street-hawkers of popular art often demand that the paintings they take on consignment be unsigned, so that they can write in their own names. These middlemen must make sure that there is no direct contact between painter and client, which would put them at a disadvantage. This principle has long been in play in Central Africa, but the painter's role in the arrangement demonstrates that what is operative here is not any notion of intellectual property but a means of profit-sharing.

Centered on the client rather than the producer, Congolese popular painting hardly facilitates the development of any notion of an idiosyncratic creative artist whose main objective is to produce his or her own unique and inimitable reflection of the world. The Congolese popular painter negotiates his vision in relation to common memory and social consciousness. He is an interpreter, and when he is successful, it is because he has managed to create an image that shows what everyone knows. His work reflects the relatively higher position of the client or buyer, while also demonstrating that this client belongs to a part of the social whole. The painter thus produces a difference that valorizes without distinguishing—that lets the client affirm his success without having to leave the group, showing him instead as the group's best representative and protector. Any

FIG. 16.
Untitled. By Fr. Amisi, 1994.
Oil on fabric, 9½ x 16¼ in. Painting made for
foreigners by Lumumbashi academy-trained artist.

radical "distinction" from the group (in the sociological sense that Pierre Bourdieu has given the term) is considered a defiant demonstration of power, and even today may be understood as an act of witchcraft that can legitimately be "counteracted" by other witchcraft moves. Only a foolhardy person would dare make himself important by taking society on. The vast majority avoid any such action, for they know that if they should fail, they risk ostracism, illness, and even death. The painting one exhibits in one's home, then, is rarely a gesture of defiance; it is far more like to be a declaration aimed at integrating one into the group as an exemplary member of it. The painters understand this, of course; they operate within this social framework and follow its rules. With rare exceptions, neither the client nor the painter wants to risk creating something that may offend the *society*. This does not imply, however, that popular painters are docile in their attitudes to the *state*.

A painter may accede to some creative freedom when working for a local client, but in such cases it is the *client* who assumes the risk of being different. (The work in question is usually bar decoration, and the freedom is expressed through risqué style and content.) It is far more common, in any case, for it to be a foreigner who offers

FIG. 17.
"Cherie, je t'en supplie, cette fois-ci, ne fais pas de jumeaux!" ["Dear, I beg you, this time, don't give birth to twins!"] By Fr. Amisi.
Watercolor on paper, 8½ x 12 in. Painting made for local public, called popular canvases.

the painter this chance. The oreigner has enormous buying power on the local market. As in the encounter with a *mamba muntu,* he is a stroke of luck that the painter must be brave enough to seize. The opportunity is fraught with danger, for success will set the painter above those with whom he shares the everyday business of surviving, and the price for this is often exclusion or exile. Chéri Samba now works exclusively for the Western market, while Tshibumba, unable to maintain his former standard of living after the departure of the foreigners who had supported him, left Lubumbashi for diamond-mining in Kasai. These two artists were given the opportunity to succeed on the external market, and had the audacity to do so. Today, both have been pushed out of the local society.

FIG. 19.
Muntu Simba. [Lion man]. By Burozi. Oil on fabric, 15 x 19 in. (a) Drawing from Burozi's notebook.

FIG. 18.
Untitled. By Fr. Amisi. Oil on fabric, 15¼ x 20¼ in. Painting made for local public, called popular canvases.

Tshibumba Kanda Matulu and the Risk of Creation

Johannes Fabian was Tshibumba's *mamba muntu.* Fabian's interest in local knowledge was the link—the *mamba muntu's* comb or mirror—that Tshibumba used to help him escape, at least temporarily, from the limitations of his condition as a local popular painter. The idea of a set of icons, touchstones of local knowledge, existed in local culture before Tshibumba, as Burozi's notebook shows. (Tshibumba worked as Burozi's apprentice in 1970–71.) The images in the notebook are not arranged in chronological order, some are only sketched roughly, while others exist only as titles. They have been arranged in categories, however, including one named "Zamani" (Past); this suggests that Burozi had an idea of something like a cycle. It was an idea he could not fully realize until 1997, when he loaned his notebook to my collaborator Michel Ntambwe; after seeing it, we commissioned him to execute all the paintings outlined in it. Burozi kept strictly to the contents of the notebook, never going beyond what a local, native clientele might request (figs. 19, 19a). In this he responded differently from Tshibumba, who almost twenty years earlier had executed about a hundred images for Fabian, all based on a dozen icons and presented in chronological—that is, historical—order (Fabian 1996). In conversations with Fabian and his Western clients of the time, Tshibumba did not hesitate to assume the role of historian (fig. 20), and, when Vincke asked him to paint what he knew about "abnormal" births (such as the birth of twins) in Luba Kasai culture, even took on that of anthropologist.

In his relations with foreigners whom he understood to be working as or like anthropologists, Tshibumba, a local wise man, adopted the position of expert, speaking as an authority to those needing instruction. And this work made him autonomous from the local society, placing him on its margins. Painters who knew him, however, say that to meet the everyday needs of his household he continued to work for the local market,

FIG. 20.
L'empire Luba de Kongolo au Shaba fut porte au Kasaï par les Baluba - Shaba qui sont devenu plutard les Baluba du Kasaï. [The Luba empire of Kongolo in Shaba was brought back to Kasai by the Baluba-Shaba, who later on became the Baluba of Kasai]. By Tshibumba, K.M., 1981. Oil on fabric, 11⁷/₈ x 19¹/₃ in.

producing multiple versions of a single icon—"The Belgian colony" or "Lumumba descending from the airplane"—and sending his son off immediately to sell them in the nearby marketplace. Of the more than 3,000 paintings that Léon Verbeek and I bought from their local owners between 1993 and 1997, more than 200 were by Tshibumba—an indication of how popular he remained with the local public.

Tshibumba adapted his themes and aesthetics to fit the two markets. He painted numerous versions of a subject called *mwa mbui* (mother of twins), for instance, but this subject is not to be found in any foreign collection, except once in the ethnographic cycle he did for Vincke (Vincke 1992). *Mwa mbui* represents a ceremony in which new-born twins are presented to the community (fig. 25). In urban Katanga it is a Luba-Kasai realm of memory that demonstrates the buyer-owner's membership in the culture. "The Belgian colony" and "Lumumba descending from the plane" by Tshibumba, on the other hand, can be found both in local homes and in the collections of foreigners (figs. 31, 60). Finally, the artist does not seem to have sold any of his "schoolbook-historical" paintings to Congolese people. It is interesting to note that while he used images to relate history, he also wrote out a history of the Congo for me, to be used by those who had no experience of the past he painted.

While certain icons uncontestably belong to *national* culture, others seem to have a local "inventor" in Katanga, credited as a master at realizing them in painting. In Lubumbashi, Tshibumba is considered such a specialist, and it often happens that paintings such as "Lumumba descending from the plane" are signed by him though executed by someone else. (The matter of the signature in local culture is too complex to discuss in detail here.) It should be noted, however, that Burozi, who presents himself (and is generally accepted) as Tshibumba's first master, affirms that these icons were *his* idea, and his notebook supports this claim. In Burozi's understanding, this gives him the right to sign Tshibumba's name to paintings Burozi himself did from his own notebook. We can say that he uses Tshibumba's signature because it sells better, even though Tshibumba was once his apprentice, and is his junior.

FIG. 21.
Mzee anakata munyororo ya utumwa. [Mzee (Kabila) is breaking the chains of suffering]. By A.B.C. Jaz, 1998. Oil on fabric, 19³/₄ x 24³/₈ in.

FIG. 22.
Le martyrs de l'independence, 4 Janvier 1959.
[Martyrs of Independence, January 4, 1959].
By Tshibumba. Oil on fabric,15½ x 28¾ in.
Tshibumba presents Lumumba as leader
of January 4, 1959 riots although he was not
directly involved.

Every painter who manages to get himself recognized as a specialist in a certain subject—
that is, who successfully sells his paintings of it on the local market—claims to have
invented it and to do it best. Tinda Lwimba, for example, claims to specialize in the figure
of the cultural hero of the Tabwa (fig. 24), an ethnic group living near Lake Tanganyika,
while Abis specializes in a hair-salon advertisement for "tresses" (fig. 15), and so forth.

Local Viewers and Political Contexts of Pictorial Memory of Lumumba

It is extremely difficult to establish a clear relation between a type of local clientele and
the production and reproduction of certain paintings. The political and social history
of the last half-century accounts for the fact that in industrial Katanga two distinct
groups have developed—the Kasaians and the Katangese—whose political interests
conflict, even though they share the same state and the same economic institutions
and conditions. Paintings presenting icons of Lumumba respond and correspond first
and foremost to Kasaian political memory.

FIG. 23.
Congolese currency, 20 makuta bill, a model
of Lumumba breaking chains paintings.

Tshibumba was the first popular painter in Katanga to use an
icon representing the legitimacy of the colonial order to depict
the Congolese people's demand for recognition of their human
dignity: the painting "The forced march of the slaves," which
is directly inspired by European engravings of the Arab slave
trade (fig. 3), from which the Belgians claimed to have delivered the Congolese. That claim was publicly rejected as early
as Lumumba's famous speech of June 30, 1960. Since then,
Congolese political culture has worked to delegitimize the
colonization with the same weapons that the Belgians used to legitimize it (fig. 26).
From 1959 to 1965, the subject and argument of all radical political discourse in Congo
was delivery from colonial slavery—breaking the chains, both symbolic and real. Even
the images of Mobutu that accompanied the grand "Roll up our sleeves" propaganda
campaign he launched at the beginning of his reign refer to this. It should be remembered that the chains of slavery set around the black prisoners' feet first appeared in
the "Belgian colony" icon.

FIG. 24.
Cultural hero of the Mfukula Tabwa
(ethnic group). By Tinda Lwimba.
Oil on fabric. 34 1/2 x 23 in.

Paintings of Lumumba appeared in Katanga in great numbers in response to particular political situations—for example just after Mobutu's coup d'état of 1965, when he was seeking the modicum of international legitimacy that he needed to allow him to hold a summit for the Organization of African Unity. Mobutu was trying to pass himself off as Lumumba's political heir. As soon as the summit was over, however, he reduced Lumumba to nothing—an empty shell, as empty as the pedestal built in Kinshasa to receive the hero's statue. The historical Lumumba was quickly confined to the archives, his memory banished from political life and his image from public space, where the only political image permissible became that of Mobutu. At the start of the 1970s, when Mobutu's "authenticity" policy put him in conflict with the Catholic Church, the dictator even tried to get himself made sacred through aesthetic means: at the beginning of every televised newscast, Zaireans now saw the effigy of their chief, the father of the national "tribe," descending from the clouds like God the Father. In the same period, Mobutu's economic "Zaireanization" policy—which took from foreigners and gave to a hand-picked group of nationals—had a terrible effect on the overall standard of living of the Katangese people. His takeover of the national economy and the ensuing embezzlement of mining revenues (corruption had always been present in the country, but it now became rife) made the old opposition between Katanga and Kinshasa painfully relevant in postcolonial Congo. It was at this time that social memory constructed a Lumumba who could stand in opposition to Mobutu, even though historically both figures were political unitarists. The opposition between the two was validated by Mobutu's known complicity in Lumumba's assassination.

The history of the recruitment of workers for the Union miniére du Haut-Katanga, the industrial enterprise that dominated Katangese economic life, explains why, from independence onward in Katanga, the political interests of workers and bosses diverged. Workers of Kasaian origin (a vague notion encompassing the Luba Kasai, the Songye, and by extension the Tetela of the former district of Lomami) understood national unity as a guarantee of their local rights. Their bosses, however, were secessionists. Meanwhile Katangese politicians sought to expel the Kasaians, whom they accused of having been allied with and benefited from the colonial system.

Mining and industrial resources and investments are concentrated in the southern part of the province of Katanga, and the dominant party in provincial politics, the Conakat, was controlled by men from that region. The northern part of the province, by contrast, where most Luba Katanga live (the Luba Katanga are culturally close to the Luba Kasai; they share the same precolonial history), favored a united Congo. Relations between the Luba Kasai

FIG. 25.
Mua Mbuyi, Saka-Yonsa.
[Mother of twins, dancing]. By Art Kande.
Oil on fabric, 13 x 19 in. Verbeek Collection.

and the Luba Katanga, though hardly free of conflict, were fairly harmonious as long as they had a common enemy in the Katangese secessionist state. As the prime minister of a united Congo who had approved sending United Nations troops to put down the secession, Lumumba was their hero. As long as the troops protected them, these two groups had to support Lumumba. For the inhabitants of eastern Kasai, on the other hand, who supported the secession of their province, Lumumba was the enemy. The memory of the Luba Kasai, expelled from Katanga to eastern Kasai, then resettled in Katanga after 1965, remained ambivalent on the subject of Lumumba until the beginning of the 1970s. It was at this time that a conception emerged of Lumumba as incarnating opposition to Mobutu—of Lumumba as the father of true independence, the independence that Mobutu had confiscated.

The attitudes of the Luba Katanga toward Lumumba have similarly fluctuated. The death of their political leader Jason Sendwe at the hands of rebels proclaiming themselves supporters of Lumumba explains this ambivalence. In the early 1970s, Mobutu used the memory of Sendwe, an anti-Tshombist and victim of the rebellion, to pit people from northern Katanga against people in the southern part of the province. But as the decade passed, growing opposition to Mobutu from all sides gave new life to memory of Lumumba.

The Songye, Luba-Katanga, and Luba-Kasai strands of urban memory diverge on the subject of Lumumba. In the 1970s, however, recollection of him emerged as a full-fledged realm of memory, since he was the only historical figure to incarnate simultaneously the struggles for dignity, modernity, and national unity. He stands in opposition not only to Mobutu but to Tshombe, the symbol of the secession. Heroes older than or contemporary with the historical Lumumba enable these different groups to appropriate the national hero (see my article elsewhere in this volume). Lumpungu II, Kabongo, and Sendwe, for example, historicize and localize (ethnicize) regional strands of memory concerning the national hero—who, in the 1970s, was also a universal hero.

It is in this context that painting, which has become the primary medium of urban memory, takes up the challenge of giving meaning to the present and representing a past that is relevant to people's understanding of the world they live in.

FIG. 26.
Je ne suis pas un homme libre.
[I am not a free man]. By Dessin Laskas.
Oil on fabric, 15½ x 22 in.

Patrice Lumumba's Youth

Jean Omasombo Tshonda

To understand the hero that Lumumba became after his death, it is worthwhile looking at what he was and did prior to his remarkable political career. Lumumba's life was one of alternating rises and falls. His courage and independence and his nearly obsessive curiosity manifested themselves at a very early age, as did his fierce determination, which could make him quite stubborn. Even as a boy he threw himself on his adversaries without trying to dodge the counterblows; he was already a political creature.

Although Lumumba had the populist style of a politician, he always lived as a loner. In any group, whether at work or play, he was always the leader. Those reluctant to submit to his domination had serious reservations about him. Lumumba left his mark on his time, but his personality remains a troubling one, difficult to grasp among the Congolese intellectuals of the period, who moved in an atmosphere charged with hatred and betrayal yet rich in friendship.

Family, Childhood, and Youth: 1925–1944

According to Lumumba's mother, Julienne Amato (interviewed in Kinshasa in 1993), and to Antoine Omatuku, the chief of Lumumba's native village, Onalua, since 1944, the birth of the boy was preceded by extraordinary natural phenomena: a shooting star, the growth of a six-crowned palm tree, an earthquake. Omatuku recounts,

> I did not personally see these things. I was born in the same period [as Lumumba], around 1923. I know of them because they have been talked about for years. We record them and they become part of our collective memory.

Many Tetela women like to speak of singular events occurring at the beginning of pregnancy, and to discover in those events signs of future happiness or misfortune. In fact the pregnancy of Lumumba's mother proceeded without medical incident. The child was born on July 2, 1925—his father, François Tolenga, noted the date on a piece of paper, according to Lumumba's younger brother, Louis Onema. But he seemed strangely marked, says his mother, and quickly became a source of astonishment, concern, and embarrassment to his relatives. Though not sickly, he manifested a sort of indolent calm that made his parents fear he was abnormal. Between the ages of seven and eleven months, when a normal child crawls along the ground toward its mother, Lumumba remained where he had been set down, a strange remoteness in his gaze. Lumumba grew up in a climate of tension and antagonism, as he stubbornly—and unsuccessfully—tried to engage and confront his relatives (he did not yet have the

FIG. 27.
Votez tous M.N.C.-L. Liste No. 4. Campagne électorale (1959) [Cast Your Vote for Lumumba. Election campaign, 1959]. By Kalume. Oil on fabric, 23¼ x 17¼ in.

29

means to do so), who he felt had rejected him. The poverty of his parents, deeper even than the general poverty of the local population, provoked in him a sense of injustice and rebelliousness. His parents separated when he was a child, and he was raised in hardship. The boy quickly took himself in hand, learning to manage alone, facing dangers and obstacles without help from others. He alone determined his life's itinerary, chosing the schools he would attend, the travels he would undertake, even the conflicts in which he would engage. Quick-minded and critical, deliberately mocking, Lumumba was unruly and often at loggerheads with those around him.

Several other factors contributed to Lumumba's difficult and turbulent youth. The history of his ethnic group—the Tetela—from the end of the nineteenth century on was marked by a series of conflicts among clans and villages. The Tetela were subjected to raids and oppression by Ngongo Leteta (born in Maniema), the agent of Swahili-speaking traders who had come by the 1870s from the east coast of Africa in search of ivory, and also of slaves to transport this precious cargo on foot. Later, in the 1880s, Ngongo freed himself from the power of his masters by allying himself with the Belgians, the new colonial power; but eventually he sought to affirm his independence of the Belgians also, and in 1893 this cost him his life. Under Ngongo's reign, several neighboring populations of different origins—Songye, Luba, and Kela, among others—were forcibly integrated into the Tetela group. When the colonial administration was faced with the problem of deciding who would succeed the chief they had eliminated (Ngongo's soldiers, incorporated into the colonial army, were beginning to revolt), it tried, without much success, to follow a similar practice: on Ngongo's death, it had separated and dispersed the populations he had united, but in 1904 it reassembled most of the inhabitants of his former capital, Kitenge Ngandu (which is in the region where Lumumba was born), creating a colonial administrative post there called Lubefu. The memory of this period is strong in Tetela historical consciousness, and among the Tetelas' neighbors, also victims of Ngongo's raids.

Witness from a young age to the problem of getting populations of diverse origins to live together, Lumumba very early on understood the importance of unity and the dangers of external intervention. Among the Tetela, contradictions in the traditional power system often allowed determined individuals to seize power without respecting the norms. Lumumba was to meet one such man, Wembo Nyama, a chief who had come from outside the region around 1902 and had managed to dominate it entirely for a brief time. (Wembo Nyama died in 1940.) In 1909, the colonial administration, which had at first enthroned Wembo Nyama as the Tetela chief, reduced his domain to the single village of Mibango, which, in 1914, was renamed Wembo-Nyama after its chief. (Lumumba attended school here for a while.) Meanwhile the first Methodist missionaries arrived, and a long period of struggle began between the Methodists and the Roman Catholic missionaries based in Tshumbe, forty kilometers away. The conflict between Protestants and Catholics (the latter supported by the colonial administration) as they competed for converts marked the history of this region and the country as a whole. The young Lumumba experienced this rivalry personally, for his village straddled the two missionary strongholds, and he attended both Protestant and Catholic schools.

Contrary to what has been said, Lumumba did not get his name from his mother. At his birth, his father named him Tasumbu, while his mother called him Tawosa, after her father. According to the catechist Ahuka, a friend of the family, he also received the Christian name Isaie. His father, a "good" monogamous Christian, would have liked the boy to become a catechist too. In fact the name Lumumba, meaning "crowd," "group," or "team in motion" in the Otetela language, was given him by one of his mother's cousins, a certain Omasase, celebrated in the region for his powers of magic. (He was said to have tamed a leopard and a boa constrictor and trained them to bring him game.) At the time Omasase gave him the name, no one paid particular attention to it. Lumumba is believed to have received the first name Patrice at baptism, while the middle name Émery is understood as a variation on the Swahili name Hemeri (Hamedi), the name of a local chief.

In his adolescence Lumumba learned to forge a personality for himself that made him very popular. And even when he wasn't liked, he knew how to get himself noticed: an extrovert, exuberant and loquacious, someone who loved to sing and dance and to express himself both verbally and physically, he stood out from other people of his age and social milieu. His restless nature kept him constantly moving—feet, arms, but also head and even eyes. In conversation, however, he could sometimes seem distracted or pensive.

Whenever the children or teenagers of Onalua had a quarrel, Lumumba was involved in it. This led to the nickname *Nyumba hatshikala okanga,* meaning "He who is always implicated."[1] In games with the other young people of the village, he had them call him Tasumbu (The she-boar's husband) and Patrice Osungu (Patrice the white). The nickname Osungu in particular contrasted radically with the boy's living conditions, his ragged clothes, and his level of education, which at the time was quite low. His ambition was deemed excessive, and made him the easy target of jokes and jeers from playmates and adults alike. Lumumba must have begun to ruminate on how he would avenge himself on fate and men.

According to Omatuku, the young Tasumbu began to be called Lumumba after a trip to Kalima, in the Maniema region: lacking official authorization to travel, he made himself a travel document, and did so in the name of Patrice Lumumba. His teachers in Wembo-Nyamba seem to remember only the name Tasumbu, though Onema affirms that he enrolled at the school there under the name Patrice Lumumba. A childhood friend named Jean Omalokenge says he was enrolled as Isaie Tasumbu Lumumba. The teacher who received him at the school in Tshumbe says he knew him as Patrice Lumumba.

Schooling

Expulsion was Lumumba's most common experience in the schools of his native area. But he is also said to have quit school twice of his own accord, because he found the level of instruction too low. He began his studies under the Catholic catechist Ahuka (there is little confirmation of the story that has him beginning school at Tshumbe). According to certain accounts, he pursued his education first with the Methodists of Wembo-Nyama, seven kilometers away, next with the Catholics at Tshumbe, twenty-eight kilometers away, and then with the Methodists again at Tunda, seventy kilometers away.

Lumumba's spoken French often lacked nasalization (a characteristic of native Otetela speakers), and it was influenced by the Methodists' standard of writing Otetela. Most of his elementary-school teachers had been trained at the English-speaking Methodist School at Wembo-Nyama, where they learned to read the French vowel *u* as "ou," and so forth.

Lumumba was baptized by the Methodists at the age of twelve in the village of Opombo. But shortly before that he was expelled from the Wembo-Nyama school for reasons that remain unclear. Georges Lory (1989) claims that the expulsion was punishment for having gotten a girl pregnant, but the Methodist pastor cited as the source of this accusation did not seem to remember it when he was interviewed in 1993. The religious and educational system itself—oppressive as it was, and from which the boy sought to dissociate himself—could have led to his being expelled for no particular reason. The director of the Methodist school, one E. H. Lovell, imposed a rigorous discipline and was not reluctant to use the whip. Boys were made to perform grueling physical tasks: crushing millet, fetching water from a spring, making and transporting bricks, building houses. Damase Wunga, the Catholic teacher who received Lumumba at Tshumbe after his expulsion by the Methodists, underlines the boy's proud and stubborn character. And the Wembo-Nyama primary school teacher Joseph

Logonya remembers.,

> Many times the pupil Lumumba set about testing the other colleagues and myself. After class, during the breaks, or in the pupils' housing area, he always had an eye out for one of us, supposedly to get us to help him read something or learn the meaning of words—mostly French—that he had written down carefully on the ground or on a piece of paper. No doubt our pupil wanted to learn, but it must also be said that this boy, with his reputation for teasing and mockery, meant to deride us; he accosted us with the purpose of embarrassing us, of proving that we were ignorant of what he seemed to know.

Lumumba spent only two trimesters at Tshumbe. According to Wunga, this was in part because his parents were too poor to buy him new clothes for his baptism, which was scheduled for the end of the year. A pupil who quit school with Lumumba explains that they left because Tshumbe was too far from the village: "We missed our games and our preserve [the village]. Tshumbe seemed rather strange to us."

In Wunga's view, Lumumba was gifted but irreverent. Wunga tells the following story: finding four spelling mistakes in a sentence a teacher had written on the board, Lumumba lost no time calling them to the teacher's attention. Humiliated, the teacher denied Lumumba's observation, and claimed that everything was correct. The disturbance created in the classroom by Lumumba's remarks came to the attention of Father Tharcisse Lazure, the headmaster. After speaking with the teacher, Father Lazure found the same mistakes that Lumumba had, but did not admit it. When Lumumba reported the incident to an inspector, Rudolph Pycke, who was passing through Tshumbe, Father Lazure became enraged and threw a ring of keys at him.[2] Lumumba and two friends of his did not return to Tshumbe after the second trimester. Interviewed in 1993, one of them claims that Lumumba said, "Let's leave this school—the teacher doesn't know anything."

Lumumba was next admitted to the school for nurses' aids at Tunda, from which he was also soon expelled. His younger brother Onema says he left the school of his own accord because the atmosphere there was stifling for a dynamic, audacious young man accustomed to village games and the company of many friends. Back from Tunda, Lumumba joined two friends who were leaving on foot for Kindu, 190 kilometers away. He had next to no money (only three francs an uncle had given him) and had to depend on his companions' generosity. He was also the only one without either a certificate of completion of elementary school or an identity booklet, and none of the boys had an official travel authorization. It was Lumumba's idea that they make themselves a travel permit on which they faked the signature of the local colonial administrator. The document had clearly been modified many times, and the signature had not been imitated very well; Lumumba had the idea of hiding these defects by touching the place where the signature was with a burning coal. The document went up in flames, and Lumumba set out without a single official document. When the three travelers arrived at Kindu, they tried to hitch a ride in a truck toward Kalima, about 120 kilometers away. The driver demanded 25 francs a head. As the two friends paid and took their places, Lumumba began to cry. Finally one of his friends gave the driver his own school certificate as a guarantee that Lumumba's fare would be paid.

On reaching Kalima, the three boys went to the colonial administration office to take care of administrative formalities. After showing their school documents, Lumumba's friends received permission to live there. For his part Lumumba produced a document that a man from his native village, Raphaël Ongendandenda, had given him,[3] but the clerk found irregularities: the first and last names of the original bearer had obviously been effaced and the name Isaie Tasumbu written in. The police commissioner himself interviewed Lumumba, in Swahili, a language the boy had not yet mastered. Lumumba responded in patchy French, managing to defend himself by inventing a story about a school director who had traveled to Makamba, near Luluabourg, leaving the school under his wife's supervision; she had given him the suspect document. Since Lumumba answered all the commissioner's questions without contradicting himself, the man decided to grant him a fifteen-day permit to stay in the city. Before that time was up, Lumumba and his friends took a math and French test. Lumumba received a score of 87 percent—compared to 53 percent and 47 percent respectively for his friends—and was hired to work for the Symétain mining company as a vendor at the canteen. As he later told friends at Kisangani, this was the beginning of a more comfortable life: for the first time, he was able to buy clothes and shoes that fit him. But after just three months on the job he was fired for poor management.

Lumumba at Stanleyville (now Kisangani)

At the end of 1944, Patrice Lumumba arrived in Stanleyville. There he lived with Paul Kimbulu, with whom he had no kinship tie, in a camp known as the "Belge," because the state-employed African clerks were housed there. Close by was the district reserved for Europeans, in which all administrative and economic activities were concentrated. Lumumba was able to to rub shoulders with *évolués,* the administration's term for "enlightened" natives (meaning educated, monogamous Christians living like whites), and with men originally from the West African coast. These people held posts in government and commerce.

Kimbulu and Lumumba had similar itineraries: both had come to Stanleyville to round out their schooling after spending time at Wembo-Nyama. Kimbulu, who arrived in 1935, four years later finished first in his class at a school for native medical assistants. For Lumumba, success came in 1948, when he finished third in his class at the Léopoldville postal school, with an overall score of 91.4 per cent. In a long letter to his friend Emile Luhahi of Wembo-Nyama, dated April 28, 1954, he explained his passion for study:

> You asked me about my future, my plans. … I have surely too many projects concentrated on and directed toward a single ideal: this is to be better and better educated, for wealth has no value for me. I would rather have an adequate education than be rich and ignorant.

> Whether or not I go to the university, I *absolutely must* bend over backwards to become a relatively educated man so as to be able to serve my homeland better. At school they give me only the instruments—it is up to me to use those instruments well, so that they will become my precious assistants. What are those instruments? They are the rudiments of knowledge we were taught on the school bench. We must now wield those rudiments, and refine them, to obtain a result superior to the one primitively acquired.

> I say to you, my dear Emile, that one can become a real university student—that is, acquire what is virtually, if not really, a university education—*at home,* if one only studies with perseverance and method. I say this through experience, experience acquired over some time. To help you really grasp the thing, I shall cite my own example. What is my previous schooling history? Surely you know it. How, then, was I able to attain my present level of education? Thanks above all to my personal effort, the work of self-perfection and perseverance.

> Today, even the Europeans describe me as someone to be reckoned with. A European friend once said to me, "All the European circles say that Lumumba wants to make his intellectual superiority felt—by the whites as well as the Congolese." This idea and this judgment are the result of the burning polemics in which I engage the Europeans in the European press, debates from which I always emerge *victorious.* Here at Stan, all the Congolese take me for a magician (which is false), while the Europeans take me for a man who has had a university education.

Many Europeans, including my supervisors at work, admit that I am more knowledgeable than many Europeans. I say all this to you without a shadow of pretension or bragadoria [sic]; I must say it to you because I consider you one of my few close friends, and so that you will be able to have a clear idea and fully appreciate how necessary the work of continuous personal self-perfection is to any being who wants to accomplish something on this earth.

As you know, there is still a question as to my pursuing university studies. I have been admitted to the University of Kimuenza [the future University Lovanium], as Monsieur Clément arranged, but this has not happened yet because of my marital situation, since there is no housing for married students. Unless I get divorced and become single again!—but that would not be suitable. It's very problematic! In any case I have not lost confidence. I will either go to the university or take correspondence courses for the same type of studies—as I've already begun to do (starting at the beginning of this month) at the Centre d'Etudes Supérieures of Brussels.

My dear Emile, with all my heart I wish you good luck in realizing your plan of going to Nivelles. Study a great deal in order to succeed when you come before the Central Board of Examiners.[4] I infinitely regret not being able to give you the information you asked for on the matter. No Black knows the questions they ask because all is *confidential*. No one here at Stanleyville has ever taken the exam for the fourth humanities category (six years of secondary-school studies required). I have no precise information that would be of interest to you. The Europeans are clever: no Black can be up on the questions they ask on the exam, because if they were, they would tell all their friends preparing for the exam so they could pass it. When are you planning to take the exam? Don't worry, I am convinced you will succeed.

Many thanks for the newspapers; I received them all. I will send you my payment for a year's subscription. Always send the newspapers by air [Lumumba's emphases throughout] (Tshonda and Verhaegen 1998:123–24).

Postal Clerk for the Colony

At Stanleyville on November 20, 1944, Lumumba signed a contract to work as a clerk for the town administration. The office he was to work in was not far from the school run by the Frères Maristes where he began taking night courses.[5] He received a monthly salary of 150 Congolese francs, plus an allowance of 75 percent of the rent for lodging "appropriate to his status." In 1947, Lumumba obtained permission to enroll in a training course at the Postal School in Léopoldville (now Kinshasa). His contract was terminated on July 6 of that year. There is no record of disciplinary infractions in his administrative file; he was considered a satisfactory employee.

On April 7, 1948, after graduating from the Postal School at Léopoldville, Lumumba was appointed third-class clerk in the Postal and Telecommunications Service for the Eastern Province. He was posted to Stanleyville, where he received a monthly salary of 1,500 francs, with a 200-franc family-support supplement and a 187.50-franc housing allowance. On October 21, 1948, he was recommended for transfer to Yangambi to train as a postmaster's assistant, and to serve as the substitute when the permanent civil servant was off-duty. On November 2 Lumumba was transferred to the post office at Yangambi.

In Stanleyville Lumumba had always been a docile clerk. Now he began to make demands. On December 8, 1948, he wrote the following complaint to the finance office:

My monthly pay is 1,840 francs minus 370 francs (taken out for an advance to buy a bicycle) = 1,470 francs. At the end of November I received 1,220 francs instead of 1470 francs. Why was all this—250 + 370 + 620 francs—taken out this time?

Furthermore, note that my housing and bicycle allowances could be maintained since my situation here is the same as in Stanleyville. The distance from my new place of residence to the office is the same as it was in Stanleyville.

Please inform me as to the deductions from my pay.

The assistant director for finances replied that his housing and bicycle allowances had indeed been discontinued, and added, in a paragraph that was crossed out but still legible, "Please inform yourself first in the future so as not to bother me with such preposterous and utterly uninteresting remarks." On December 31, Lumumba once again claimed a bicycle allowance but failed to obtain it. Starting in May 1950, however, he was paid a monthly housing allowance of 187.50 francs. (On April 3 of that year, he had been ordered to go to Stanleyville to have his vision tested; he had left Yangambi on April 14.) Until 1956 the administrative file on him primarily concerned two loan requests: one to the extracustomary center[6] in Stanleyville for the construction of a house (the loan amount was first fixed at 50,000 francs but went up to 125,000 francs), the other a request for 6,000 francs to buy furniture: refused. As for his professional work, Lumumba was rated "good" by his immediate superior.

A bill dated January 20, 1950, states that Lumumba "owes the colonial treasury the sum of 179.84 francs, the amount of the deficit observed by inspectors and reported on December 8, 1949." Then on July 20 of the same year he was fined a sum equivalent to half his salary over an eight-day period on the following charge: "Having seriously violated administrative instructions and rules several times for his own benefit; not having replied to summons for explanation addressed to him by the administrator of the territory of Isangi; and having used roundabout means to make it seem that he had." In 1956 these points became the subject of a trial. At that time Lumumba affirmed, "I had ordered a parcel for which payment was not made on reception, and I took the parcel before making that payment. That's why I got all these criticisms." Chief Inspector Bastin gives another story: Lumumba was transferred from the post office at Yangambi "because he had taken money from the cash box in exchange for a transfer of funds from his own bank account—funds that he did not have." Accused of embezzling 56,550 francs, Lumumba was officially fired on July 4, 1956. Two days later—on July 6, 1956—he was arrested.

Lumumba's Associative Activities

When while Lumumba was a postal worker, he became renowned in Stanleyville for his newspaper articles and the important positions he occupied in various associations. Between 1948 to 1956, Lumumba wrote a total of seventy-four texts for *La Croix du Congo* and *La Voix du Congolais*. He also wrote articles for the *Bulletin de l'église méthodiste du Congo central*, published at Wembo-Nyama. He was a member of the Association des évolués de Stanleyville (AES), the Association des anciens élèves des Pères Scheut (Association of former students of the Scheut Fathers), the Amicale des postiers indigènes de la Province orientale (Club for native postal workers of the Province Orientale), the Association du personnel auxiliaire indigène de la colonie (Association of native auxiliary colony personnel), the Fédération des associations de Stanleyville, and the Union belgo-congolaise de Stanleyville. He also volunteered to supervise the Public Library for Congolese, and there drew up a list of persons desiring to take courses with the Frères Maristes to prepare for Central Board examinations.

Of all Lumumba's functions, the most important was that of president of the AES. He became secretary of the organization in 1952, vice-president in 1953, and finally president in March 1954, holding the position until December 1955. Lumumba's strategy since 1952 had been to criticize the management of the AES in order to win the members' trust. Once at the head of the organization, he worked with manifest enthusiasm: with the support of certain well-known Europeans, he made the AES into an effective instrument for putting pressure on the colonial administration, meanwhile winning the sympathy and support of the general public by organizing various festivities and theatrical productions. For the first time, the main objective of the AES was *not* merely to obtain special status and privileged living conditions for the *"évolués."* The masses were no longer considered with disdain or contempt. Lumumba spoke to the people of the local extracustomary town in their own vernacular, and organized theatrical productions staging scenes of indigenous life.

When a declaration from the Appeals Court of Léopoldville arrived on August 5, 1954, officially recognizing Lumumba as an *"immatriculé,"*[7] his prestige in the eyes of the *évolués* and his self-confidence in relation to the Europeans were greatly reinforced. Among the reasons given for the judgment we may read the following: Lumumba "has engaged in sustained social and intellectual activity, working with indigenous groups and intellectuals and publishing articles in three periodicals." Mr. Songolo, then secretary of the AES, sent a letter praising Lumumba to the journal *L'Afrique et le monde* (published in Brussels), expressing "recognition of the marked competence, tact, understanding, and good-naturedness with which [Lumumba] has led the Association des évolués of Stanleyville."[8] The letter was published in full, together with a photo of Lumumba.

A few months later, however, Songolo would play a central role in removing Lumumba from the presidency of the association.

In November of 1954, the directorial committee of the AES took advantage of the Belgian Colonial Minister August Buisseret's visit to Stanleyville to request that "indigenous organizations be consulted when representatives of indigenous populations are appointed to organizations and councils called upon to participate in government."[9] On behalf of the *évolués,* Lumumba presented the minister with a letter of grievance concerning the racial discrimination practiced by administration "underlings" and "the lower echelons of colonial settlers and tradesmen." He then evoked the creation of a "Belgian-Congolese community, which would cement for eternity the brilliant work of our great liberator, Léopold II."[10] In June of the following year, when the Belgian King Baudouin visited Stanleyville, Lumumba spoke with him twice. These exchanges produced no concrete results, but greatly reinforced Lumumba's prestige and self-confidence. Nonetheless, the AES committee members had great difficulty accepting Lumumba's initiatives with Buisseret, and the prominent role he had begun to play. Among other things, they reproached him for sending—without consulting them first—a telegram of thanks to the minister on behalf of the AES for the establishment of nonreligious schools. This was considered an abuse of power. On July 5, 1955, the committee wrote to Lumumba to "warn [him] not to engage in such intrigues." He was criticized for his dictatorial "style" of action, his personal ambition, the fact that he did not consult the committee, and his tendency to take unpredictable initiatives.[11]

The king's visit in June of 1955, and the colonial minister's visit to Lumumba's home at the same time, became the objects of bitter and stormy debate, leading the committee to denounce its president's "serious breaches of propriety." Lumumba was reproached for "his loquacity before H.M. the King," as well as for "the gestures accompanying his torrent of words."[12] After Buisseret's reception at Lumumba's home, moreover, Lumumba is said to have asked to accompany the minister in his official car. The committee concluded, "Obviously the minister could not refuse, but it will readily be imagined how impolite this was!"[13] Finally Lumumba was criticized for refusing to accept the presence of local authorities—leaders of the extracustomary center—at the reception for the minister; nor was Father Jansen, counselor to the AES, invited to attend. Since Lumumba

Fig. 1.
Lumumba en prison sous garde d'un militaire congolais [Lumumba in prison under guard of the Congolese military]. By Tinda Lwimba, ca. 1980s. Oil on cotton, 20¼ x 15 in. (See Frontspiece).

had praised the minister for establishing secular schools, this could only be seen as another slap in the face for the Catholic Church.

All this would probably not have sufficed to get Lumumba's presidency of the association revoked had his financial management not been called into question. On December 23, 1955, the assembly voted to remove Lumumba from the presidency. Though he had been forbidden on this occassion to address the assembly, the committee later relented and gave him permission to do so. At the podium, instead of reading a report he had prepared, Lumumba gave a conciliatory speech, demonstrating his capacity to adapt and improvise.

Lumumba's departure from the presidency of the AES consolidated the triumph of the moderate faction of the *évolués*. This split in 1955 prefigured those of 1959 and 1960. (Though certain of Lumumba's opponents in the AES would join his Mouvement National Congolais (MNC) in 1959, their support would not last very long.) The division between the two camps was not yet ideological, however, but was provoked by Lumumba's personality, style of action, and choice of alliances.

Leaving the presidency of the AES enabled Lumumba to get himself accepted in liberal colonial circles; he maintained his privileged relations with Minister Buisseret and developed ties with several Belgian politicians. This led him to believe he need pay no attention to subordinate colonial authorities—until the day they caught him out for breaking the law.

Arrest and Imprisonment

The local colonial administration had been watching Lumumba since the beginning of 1956, but he did not take the appropriate precautions, believing that his connections in high places were protection enough. He even went so far as to criticize the local authorities, and all who collaborated with them, in public. On July 6, 1956, then, on his return from a two-month visit to Belgium, where he had been invited along with fifteen other important Congolese personalities, Lumumba was arrested for embezzling the sum of 126,000 Belgian francs (about $3,000) while working as a civil servant in the post office. He confessed and was sentenced to two years in prison. His status as an *immatriculé* permitted him to be tried before the Tribunal de première instance (a court for whites), but the conditions of his detention and the severity of the sentence were quite disproportionate to the crime. It was clear to all in Stanleyville that Lumumba's opponents, both white and black, were seizing the chance to humiliate him socially and cast him down. On appeal, the sentence was reduced to eighteen months, and then, with Buisseret's intercession, to twelve. Buisseret also reimbursed Lumumba's debt to the administration.

Lumumba's imprisonment only increased his popularity. With the exception of a few zealous servants of the colony, the Congolese did not consider it an indignity to be caught despoiling the colonial occupant. The injustices committed against the colonized had become so flagrant that they made what the colonizer considered common-law crimes appear to the people as feats of prowess.

During his stay in prison (fig. 1), Lumumba wrote *Le Congo, terre d'avenir, est-il menacé?* (Is the Congo, land of the future, in danger?). It has been said that the book was a kind of ransom he paid for his early release. Once out of prison, Lumumba never mentioned the book, and it was only published after his death.

Fig. 42.
*1er arrestation, Lumumba en 1959, à Buluo
la Prison Central de Jadotville* [1st Arrest,
Lumumba in 1959 at Buluo Central Prison
at Jadotville). By Tshibumba, K.M.
Oil on fabric, 14¼ x 22 in.(See p. 72)

Conquering Léopoldville

During the year he spent at Bracongo, Lumumba engaged in significant political activity.
He became vice-president of the Cercle libéral d'études et d'agrément (Liberal study and
leisure circle), thereby consolidating his ties with an important faction of the colonial
administration. This group, with the support of the liberal Minister Buisseret, sought
to act as a counterweight to the influence of the clergy. Nor did he neglect the other
centers of political activity, becoming a member of the Centre d'études et de recherches
sociales, the group out of which the *"Conscience africaine"* manifesto had developed.
In this group Lumumba represented the liberal organizations.

While Lumumba was in prison, important events occurred in Léopoldville. There, on
August 23, 1956, the Association des Bakongo (ABAKO), which had begun acting as
a political party, published a manifesto in response to a text by Congolese Catholic
intellectuals, *"Conscience africaine"* (African consciousness).[14] From now on, the political
future would be determined in the capital, as Lumumba clearly understood: when he
left prison, in June of 1957, he settled in Léopoldville. Here, on the recommendation of
liberal friends, he was hired as sales manager of the Bracongo brewery. The job suited
him well because it enabled him to get acquainted with the entire city of Léopoldville.

Conscious of the importance of ethnic affiliation, Lumumba managed to outrun several
important Tetela figures—even though they enjoyed the considerable advantages of
seniority and the support of the colonial authorities—to become the president of the
Fédération des Batetela of Léopoldville. The Fédération broke up shortly after, however,
and Lumumba had in the meantime made some implacable enemies within his own
ethnic group. This political scenario, which had already been played once at Stanleyville,
would be replayed later with the Mouvement National Congolais.

The founding of the MNC on October 8, 1958, was preceded by several political events
that accelerated the development of political consciousness among the urban elites,
particularly in Léopoldville. The local elections of December 1957, which brought victory
to ABAKO, were characterized by ethnic confrontation. On April 20, 1958, Joseph
Kasa-Vubu—the president of ABAKO, and the elected "bourgmestre" (mayor) for
the municipality of Dendale—demanded "internal autonomy" and the institution of a
"Congolese nationality." At Brazzaville in the French Congo on August 26, the French
leader Charles de Gaulle promised independence to those French colonies in Africa
who wanted to take it.

Lumumba had not been much of a presence on the political scene during this period,
but at the end of August 1958 he and sixteen other Léopoldville figures signed an open
letter to the new minister of the Belgian Congo, protesting the absence of Congolese
on the task-force committee established to prepare a study of the colony's political
problems. The signatories demanded general elections to "constitute a government that
will be accountable to the country." Above all, they rejected the federalism that had
been "called for recently by separatists more concerned with their personal interests
than with the future of their country."

There is no indication that Lumumba had a decisive role in formulating this text. He
did, however, play an important role in the creation of the MNC. The party, which
assembled the most important of the capital's unitarist nationalists (supporters of a
single, united nation as opposed to a federation), was headed by a committee that
included representatives of the largest ethnic groups in Léopoldville; its goal was to
present a united front against the Belgian government's task force and the ABAKO
federalists. No one as yet occupied the presidency of this committee, and Lumumba
simply named himself to it in a communiqué. He was accepted because of his talents as
an orator and his long experience working for local associations. The weakness of the
other committee members, the differences among them, and Lumumba's lack of a clear

and complete political program (which might have provoked opposition) enabled him to lead the MNC without sharing power.

In July of 1959, Lumumba both demanded immediate independence and attacked the federalists as black colonialists put in place by the colonizing power. Now that independence had been virtually attained, the political struggle changed: it was no longer the colonizer who had to be eliminated, but the political competition. As early as July 17, however, the MNC split into two wings, one—Lumumba's—defending a radical nationalist stance, the other, more moderate, led by Albert Kalonji, Joseph Ileo, and Joseph Ngalula. The contest turned in favor of Lumumba's MNC—called the MNC-L—for many reasons, including Lumumba's dynamism and talent; his network of collaborators and of devoted and compliant activists; and the solidarity of the Tetela.

Second Arrest and Rise to Power

An event at the end of October 1959 almost upset Lumumba's political career again: riots broke out during the MNC congress in Stanleyville, and fourteen people were killed as the colonial army put down the turbulence. Lumumba, presiding over the party congress, violently attacked Belgium and called for a boycott of the December elections. The radicalism of his speech anticipated that of June 30, 1960; in both cases the Belgians could not forgive him, and he was arrested and sentenced to six months in prison (fig. 42). Once again, however, luck was with him, and he was released to participate in the Belgian-Congolese Round Table talks in Brussels. It was at these talks that independence was agreed to, and scheduled for June 30, 1960. Lumumba sensed victory approaching.

General elections were set for May 20. That did not leave much time to catch up with the ethnic and regional parties, overcome the obstacles placed by the colonial administration, train party cadres and militants, and above all compensate for the masses' lack of political consciousness and training. During the pre-election period, Lumumba and his MNC campaigned tirelessly (fig. 28). In the first four months of 1960, the profile of

FIG. 28.
Lumumba dans un village meeting - tres grave.
[Lumumba at a very serious village meeting].
By Tinda Lwimba. Oil on fabric, 15¹/₂ x 23¹/₂ in.

Fig. 29.
Le 30 Juin 1960, Zaire Indépendant
(Zaire Independence, June 30, 1960). By
Tshibumba M. Oil on fabric, 17³/₄ x 24⁵/₈ in.
Bol Collection.

a radical nationalist and unitarist politician became clearly discernible, a man of extreme combativeness and courage, a powerful orator but also a demagogue, a flexible, effective tactician who could blow hot and cold, alternating alliance-making with demands for unconditional acceptance.

Lumumba's party won 41 seats out of 137. After the failure of every maneuver to delay, he was elected prime minister; Joseph Kasa-Vubu was elected president. The Congo became an independent nation on June 30, 1960. Lumumba marked the day with a radical, impassioned speech before the Belgian king and the newly elected Congolese Parliament (fig. 29). In it he came back to what he had often proclaimed to African audiences, to what was in reality the content of his childhood memories: the miserable poverty of the colonized peasants, and the violence of the colonizer.

1. *Nyumba* is an aromatic plant growing close to where people live. There are many popular beliefs about it, namely that it has the power to keep away bad spirits (witches). The Tetela use *nyumba* to prepare a variety of therapeutic potions.

2. In 1964, Father Lazure was roughed up by Simba rebels in reprisal for this incident.

3. Raphaël Ongendandenda worked at the Symétain, a mining company, where Lumumba himself was soon to be hired.

4. The Belgian colonial system allowed self-taught African students, persons who had not attended school, to come before a Central Board of Examiners. If they passed the exams, they could then be admitted to an institution of higher education.

5. The information in this section of the essay comes from the "Lumumba" file in the National Archives, Kinshasa. The Frères Maristes were one of several Catholic congregations active in the Belgian Congo, and specialized in education.

6. In many urban centers and cities the African population, living in segregated quarters, was put under special administration of an African chief who was himself supervised by a colonial officer. This administrative arrangement was called *extra-coutumier* (extracustomary).

7. The "immatriculés" were a special category of natives who were granted civil rights similar to the those of the whites. They could travel first-class with white passengers, had access to white theaters, and, as quite another type of privilege, were not subject to whipping in prison.

8. *L'Afrique et le monde* 39 (September 30, 1954).

9. Statement of the AES delegation, Stanleyville, November 9, 1954.

10. *L'Afrique et le monde* 49 (December 9, 1954).

11. AES committee memo on Lumumba's destitution of duty, n.d., p. 3. The committee wrote, "Your vanity, your boastfulness, your haughty manners and exaggerations mean that you choose to consider your fellows inferior beings" (p. 1).

12. Ibid, p. 2. Some speculate that Lumumba had displeased certain colonial officials, who then put pressure on the *évolués* to repudiate him; interview with Baelongandi conducted by H. Weiss, Stanleyville, 1960. Courtesy of H. Weiss.

13. AES committee memo on Lumumba's destitution of duty, p. 3.

14. These manifestos were the first public documents by native intellectuals to call for an end to racial segregation and to discuss the future of the country in terms of independence.

LE CONGO EST EN TROUBLE A CAUSE DE CET HOMME DE LUMUMBA ARRETONS LE

Patrice Lumumba at the Crossroads of History and Myth

Nyunda ya Rubango

A few months before his death, Patrice Lumumba prophetically declared, "For the people I have no past, no parents, no family. I am an idea" (Legum 1966:xi). This statement was meant to exonerate him of various ethnic and racial grievances and to justify the weaknesses of his failing government. It also contended that nationalist ideals superseded personal, regional, and ethnic interests. Yet by foregrounding his rootlessness, Lumumba betrayed his awareness of his historicity as a leader.

Political Action

Lumumba's very short period of office was an endless calvary. On a daily basis he faced the multiple aspects of the Congolese crisis: the mutiny of the army (the Armée nationale congolaise, or ANC), the incursion of Belgian troops, the rupture of the country's diplomatic relations with the former colonial power, the secession of two strategically important mining provinces (Katanga and South Kasai), ethnic and regional tensions all over the country, economic and administrative disasters, the inefficient and improper intervention of United Nations (U.N.) troops, conflicts resulting from the cold war, and institutional impasse. Lumumba's decline was even greater and more rapid than his ascent. After winning the confidence of all the nationalist parties, leaders, and regions, and the sympathy of a good portion of the Parliament, he was condemned to face numerous internal and external enemies. He was accused, or suspected, of compromising sacred Western interests. He lost most, if not all, of his popularity in hostile areas, including the capital as well as the separatist provinces. He was daily abandoned or betrayed by powerful national friends and allies. He was at odds with U.N. representatives in both Léopoldville and New York, and even some of his few defenders, such as President Kwame Nkrumah of Ghana and other African leftist leaders, accused him of extremism—of lacking tolerance, realism, and patience. His military and political power was diminished. His efforts to maintain the integrity of the national territory, to administer and develop the young nation, and to ensure the security of persons and properties proved relatively vain. His statements and policies were vehemently criticized. Yet he sustained a strong faith in the legitimacy of his nationalist action, until a national conspiracy, evidently inspired and even financed from outside, expelled him from the political arena and ended his life.

The institutional crisis brewed at the beginning of September 1960. On September 5, President Joseph Kasa-Vubu and Prime Minister Lumumba respectively dismissed each other from office. Nine days later, Colonel Joseph-Désiré Mobutu, a former friend of

FIG. 30.
Le Congo est en trouble a cause de cet homme de Lumumba. Arretons le. [Congo is in trouble because of this man, Lumumba. Arrest him.]. By Burozi, signed Tshibumba. Oil on fabric, 18 x 13 in.

FIG. 31.
Lumumba arriving in Elisabethville (Torment).
By Burozi, signed Tshibumba.
Oil on fabric, 12¾ x 22½ in.

Lumumba's and the man in effect running the army (as commanding officer of the headquarters in Léopoldville), "neutralized" both authorities. In principle, Mobutu actually "neutralized" all of the executive and legislative branches, but in practice only Lumumba and his faithful friends and cabinet were the victims of this masquerade. On September 7, the Chamber of Deputies reconfirmed both Kasa-Vubu and Lumumba in office, and the following day the Senate too reconfirmed Lumumba; but a coup de théâtre, if not a mere coup, was in view.

On September 20, Mobutu installed in power the "Collège des Commissaires Généraux," formed for the most part of young college students, new graduates, and technicians, and led by Justin Bomboko. The Collège completely supplanted the legal government and worked in relative harmony with Kasa-Vubu, who remained in office. It had a double mission: to resolve the general chaos and to protect the Congo from "Communist colonialism and Marxist-Leninist imperialism." It remained in power until February of 1961.

In Kinshasa, the capital, Lumumba was not only the black sheep to be removed from power but an embarrassing, even dangerous presence that had to be eradicated at all cost. First came a judicial attempt to dismiss or "neutralize" him—to curb his ability to act. Although Lumumba was theoretically protected by parliamentary immunity, on October 10, 1960, he was confined to house arrest, guarded by both ANC and U.N. soldiers. In a message of December 7 to the U.N. secretary general, Kasa-Vubu charged him with five main grievances: usurpation of public functions; violation of individual liberty by physical torture; attacks on state security; organization of hostile groups with the goal of causing ruin, massacre, or pillage; and inciting the military to commit infractions. In response, all of Lumumba's worst enemies called for a trial.

The fallen prince lost all hope of a *retour en force* to the capital when the U.N. General Assembly recognized Kasa-Vubu's representation as legitimate. His only hope in the short term lay in his desperate quest to reach his bastion in Province Orientale. On November 27, then, Lumumba escaped from his guarded residence—but after four days of successful crusade through Kwilu and Kasai, he was arrested in Mweka by Mobutu's military. He was then handed over in Port-Franqui to Gilbert Pongo, who had commanded the pursuit. Instead of reaching Stanleyville, where he intended to rebuild his power (with the support of the Gizenga-Lundula government), Lumumba was brought back to the capital on December 2 and returned to Mobutu. The next day he was transferred to Camp Hardy, in Thysville, where he was detained with nine leaders of his faction, including Maurice Mpolo and Joseph Okito.

In either Léopoldville or Thysville, Lumumba remained politically dangerous, even confined in prison. Accordingly Mobutu, security chief Victor Nendaka, and members of the Collège decided to move him away, and on January 17, 1961, he, Mpolo, and Okito were transferred to Elisabethville, capital of Katanga. (fig. 31) (The dissident Mouvement National Congolais [MNC] leader Albert Kalonji had requested that he be sent for trial to the South Kasai capital of Bakwanga, site of a massacre by troops acting under Lumumba's name earlier in the year; but it was to Elisabethville that he was sent, supposedly to ensure the integrity of the trial and the secure detention of the three prisoners.) Lumumba was obviously a precious commodity. There were rumors of a plan between Kinshasa, Elisabethville, and Bakwanga: Lumumba was to be the sacrifice paid to reunify the nation.

A meaningful "coincidence": the Congolese escort for the three prisoners happened to be ethnically homogenous (Luba Kasai). It was composed of three guards (who brutally mistreated the bound prisoners during the entire flight) and two commissioners, Ferdinand Kazadi and Jonas Mukamba. There was little chance of mercy, breach of secrecy, or disagreement, then, during this delicate operation. Furthermore, the Elisabethville authorities had developed a deep hatred for the man whose centralism, unitarism, and even "Communism" blocked their "independence". It was said that the local government regretted only the danger of "soiling the Katangese land" with the blood of this human, moral, and political "wreck." So Lumumba "disappeared," both physically and figuratively: he died and left no traces in Katanga; he was hopefully silenced forever (fig. 32). According to persistent rumors (so far not contradicted), his body and those of Mpolo and Okito were dissolved in a bath of sulfuric acid. Historically one thing is certain: the alleged trial never took place; the three prisoners perished in Elisabethville on the night of their arrival there, on January 17, 1961; their bodies were mysteriously destroyed to prevent the possibility of pilgrimages, or of reprisals, by followers and admirers; all tracks were covered to forestall any local, national, international, or U.N. investigation.

Lumumba disappeared physically, but he left behind a discourse, an idea, an ideology. He entered both history and myth.

FIG. 32.
Bodies of Lumumba, Mpolo, and Okito. By Burozi. Oil on fabric, 15¼ x 19½ in. See fig. 67.

Discourse, Idea, and Ideology

As a young man, Lumumba was a correspondent for La Croix du Congo, La Voix du Congolais, Le Stanleyvillois, and L'Afrique et le monde, and the editor of L'Echo postal. He excelled very soon, then, in writing articles for indigenous newspapers and magazines. From 1950 to 1956, most of his writings were conciliatory, and focused on the theme of colonialism: more than once he praised "the grand civilizing works initiated by the Belgians." In a historical homage to Sir Henry Morton Stanley written in 1954, he glorified not only the "incomparable explorer" but King Léopold II, the founder of Belgium's colonial empire, and all the pioneers of Belgian colonization who had "delivered" the Congolese from "atavistic fear," "famines," and "devastating epidemics." He praised these Europeans for having brought "to a country plunged in an unhappy barbarism the benefits of civilization," freedom, and human dignity and welfare; these men even "built our intelligence" and "make our souls progress." For the young columnist, the Congolese were simply "pupils" of Belgium, "small young brothers" "to be guided, brought up, led to the emancipated future."

Even though Lumumba admired the colonial and missionary order, he did criticize Belgian rule to some extent: he pleaded for a better integration of the African population, and especially of the elite; he defended the cause of the wretched masses; he called for a harmonious "Belgian Congolese Community"; he implored the colonial administration to show a better grasp of indigenous problems; he put special emphasis on education and the condition of women; he preached to fellow évolués the virtues of patriotism, integrity, hard work, professionalism, education, a sense of responsibility, politeness, etc.; and he cultivated a moderate discourse (Verhaegen 1993, Rubango 1997). But when he wrote for colonial publications, Lumumba presented the image of an African elite who believed in the supremacy of Western technology and culture. He seemed a docile, grateful, and thoughtful subject.

FIG. 33.
Lumumba with Congolese delegation at the Brussels roundtable to discuss Congo independence. Signed Tshibumba. Oil on canvas, 19¹/₂ x 28 in. Verbeek Collection.

Congo, terre d'avenir, est-il menacé, a posthumous essay of Lumumba's published in 1961 but written in prison in 1956, is a combination of colonial saga, nationalist criticism of colonialism, and conciliatory statements on the Belgian presence in the Congo—an ambivalence it preserves throughout. Lumumba develops a typically colonialist discourse in assuming that colonization is humanitarian in principle, made up of "sacrifices" and committed to the "civilization" of Africans in their indescribable "abyss." He praises the colonialists who have made the Congolese a "free, happy, strong, and civilized people"; Belgians, he says, have restored the "human dignity" of the Congolese, ending the slave trade, epidemics (especially of the sleeping sickness), and "savage practices." He also pays fulsome tribute to "His Majesty" King Baudouin, "our beloved king"—even while he simultaneously honors all "friends" and "defenders" of blacks, and all "pioneers of the Independent State." When Lumumba argues that "the Congo is worth nothing without whites" (though even more worthless without blacks), and when he requests, from a bourgeois point of view, the total integration of the African elite alone, he is cultivating a conciliatory discourse. In so writing, during the most triumphant days of Belgian imperial conquest, he is developing the expressions and ideas of his time. Even while they sought privilege, influence, and power, the African elite were extremely alienated; they were infused with a sense of the absolute cultural inferiority of their continent and race in relation to Europe and the West. They were encouraged in this belief by Belgium's "paternalism," its educational methods and principles and its system of rigid censorship. The peaceful "model colony" happened also to be the "empire of silence" vividly depicted by reporter O. P. Gilbert (1947).

Lumumba's essay is dualistic in its effort both to support the Belgian colonial regime and to supply it with positive criticism. In a progressive vein, Lumumba demands a number of political rights, the integration of the Congolese population, fair pay, labor, justice, education, the freedom to travel, the abolition of all forms of racial and social discrimination, the promotion of the Congolese woman, and new, fair policies and laws on jails, health, leisure, land ownership, and immigration. He also demands a more realistic approach to Congolese problems, more-human racial relations, respect for African "authenticity" (sic) and tradition, the Africanization of executive positions, and preparation of the elite who would run the nation after emancipation.

Great events came in 1958. Social reforms introduced by the liberal minister August Buisseret shaped people's expectations. Freedom of expression and thought began to be a reality. A free, independent African press emerged. Cultural and political associations, formerly considered taboo or questionable, were allowed to exist. Major political parties were formed. The Brussels World's Fair extended the framework of previous visits of Congolese officials to Belgium; Congolese leaders and *évolués* were brought to Belgium as showpieces for the Congolese pavilion, and both Congo's masses and its elite discovered another face of colonialism. Lumumba and other leaders came in contact with progressive and liberal Belgian groups (including "Les Amis de Présence Africaine," a group notably including Jean Van Lierde). He met members of leftist parties and organizations, and delegates from better-assimilated French colonies that were evolving in a more open atmosphere (fig. 33). For Lumumba, the climax of this year was his participation in the Pan-African Conference in Accra that December. In addition to sealing some precious friendships, such as those with Nkrumah, Sékou Touré of Guinea, Gamal Abdel Nasser of Egypt, Frantz Fanon, and others, he espoused the ideas of unconditional and immediate emancipation, anticolonialism, antiimperialism, African sovereignty, liberty, solidarity, unity, dignity, positive neutrality, and so on, all typical mottoes of the Pan-African faith and ideologies that would sustain his political struggle, thought, and actions from the late 1950s up to his fall and martyrdom.

Lumumba's speech on Independence Day—June 30, 1960—centered on nationalism (fig. 35). To say the least about this controversial speech, it was a reaction to a complex series of facts. First, it answered the respectively moderate and paternalistic speeches of

President Kasa-Vubu and King Baudouin. Some analysts therefore have advanced the hypothesis that it was to some extent improvised, and in fact it was not scheduled on the program; Lumumba wrote it—especially the uncivil part—after receiving copies of the earlier speeches, and he was probably influenced, in part or in whole, by his radical friends and counselors. In the speech, Lumumba openly voiced his accumulated anger. He celebrated national sovereignty as the victory of Congolese nationalism over Belgian and European imperialism. Before preaching patriotism to his fellow "victorious" citizens, he also vehemently denounced the vices, excesses, violence, contradictions, injustices, and weaknesses of colonial rule (McKown 1969:101–4).

This discourse would not have surprised an audience familiar with the anticolonialism apparent in some of Lumumba's writings and speeches of the preindependence period. His poem *"Pleure, o Noir frère bien-aimé"* ("Weep, o Beloved Black Brother," 1959) is an excellent illustration of his new vision (fig. 34). In writing indebted to the lyric tone of the poetry of Negritude, Lumumba laments the sad lot of the black man throughout history; but this moving prayer ends with absolute faith in emancipation, dignity, and joy.

Western critics were unanimous on the heavy consequences of Lumumba's historic speech, and on its inadequacy. Generally labeled "profane," "iconoclastic," and " irresponsible," it was also said to break the elementary rules of decency and diplomacy, since the audience included the king and other distinguished international guests, and since it was pronounced on the very day of independence. Most writings on the subject record this act as Lumumba's first major political error, the source of his fall and even of his death. It has been taken to illustrate the aggressiveness, animosity, hypocrisy, racism, and lack of common sense, even insanity, of a controversial leader essentially identified as a rebel and rabble-rouser.

Paradoxically, however, many later-famous anti-Lumumbist activists and writers recognized the "truth" of Lumumba's speech at the time. In crucial respects, too, Lumumba has in retrospect proved himself realistic: he never harbored illusions about "the other face" of the thrilling *"Dipanda,"* *"Uhuru,"* or *"Kimpwanza"* (three words for "independence") (fig. 35), and he contended that hard times preceded the regaining of the lost "paradise." The Congolese people, he believed, would have to work hard and "tighten their belts" (at least for a while), since money, abundance, and prosperity, unlike manna, did not miraculously fall from heaven, but were the products of continuous effort.

Even when storms shook relations between the Belgian and Congolese governments, or when he was in detention in Camp Hardy, Lumumba made no cheap, open show of racism or xenophobia, collective, public, or individual. The leitmotifs of his arguments on the types of relationships that had to be brought into being between the former colony and the former colonial power were peace, collaboration, harmony, and mutual respect. This was true even of the popular speeches he directed to his most faithful and fanatical political clientele. The moderate, conciliatory addresses he delivered in Sankuru and Luluabourg in September 1959 and in Stanleyville in July 1960 are particularly eloquent. No honest critic would contest the pacific, humanitarian, and "responsible" tone of the appeal broadcast to the Belgian community on June 29, 1960: among other attributes of the emancipation of the young nation, Lumumba called for calm, fraternity, the security of persons and properties, and the collaboration of both the European and the African communities.

FIG. 34.
Allegory of Lumumba signing Declaration of Independence. By Morgan, 1995. Oil on fabric, 19 x 14½ in.

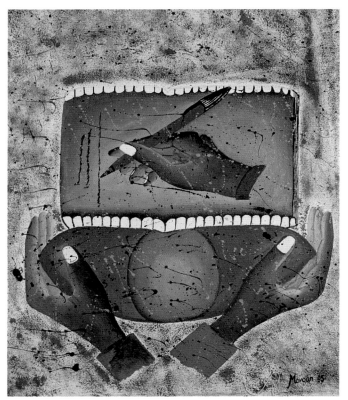

Fig. 35.
Le 30 Juin 1960. [The 30th June 1960
(Independence Day)]. By Tshibumba.
Oil on fabric, 19½ x 27 in. Verbeek Collection.

Lumumba was obviously a direct, partisan inheritor of the revolutionary Pan-African ideologies. Without taking these into account, it is impossible to grasp the Jacobinism of his thought and action—his naive and desperate quest for dignity, liberty, "positive neutrality," solidarity, unity, a strong centralized government, compromise of the interests of the political aristocracy, altruism, care for the masses, the political courage for heroism and martyrdom, and so on. Lumumba's entire mission was founded in sacrifice. "If I have sacrificed everything (my position, my family, my leisure), it is in order to serve our fatherland," he told his friend Van Lierde (1972:99).

Lumumba's ideology can be evaluated not only in his writings, speeches, and statements but through the profile and history of his party. Although his MNC drew many of its members from a relatively marginalized city (Stanleyville, the third biggest city in the Congo) and relied significantly on ethnic support (among the Anamongo group), it was the only nationwide nationalist party in the country. The rival Parti National du Progrès (PNP) was nationwide as well, yet anything but nationalist. The MNC was launched as a study group, "the outgrowth of the manifesto of *Conscience Africaine*" (Lemarchand 1964:197). When it grew into a political party, it defined its objectives in the following terms: to achieve independence immediately, completely, and nonviolently; to establish democratic structures; to secure the fundamental liberties guaranteed by the Universal Declaration of the Rights of Man; to end colonialism and imperialism; to defend national unity; to combat ethnic and regional separatism; to establish a liberal economy; to carry out a social policy ensuring full employment and welfare, and especially favoring education, health, the condition of women, and youth activities; to protect and promote Congolese arts and cultures; and to secure respect for African tradition.

FIG. 36.
Allegory of Congolese struggle for independence,
Lumumba and Mulele. By Morgan, 1995.
Oil on fabric, 11¾ x 16¾ in.

Lumumba was accused of idiosyncrasy and impulsiveness, and of lacking not only a concrete social and economic policy but realism, tolerance, stability, and planning. Yet some facts speak eloquently: his disapproval of the incursion by Belgian troops; his determination to defend the national borders at all costs, and to combat tribalism and separatism, especially the secessions in Katanga and South Kasai; his plans for administrative, economic, educational, and salary policies; his concern for economic emancipation; his commitment to the unity and liberation of all of the African nations; his attempts to decolonize the consciousness of African people, and to establish a new cultural and social order; and so on. This short-lived leader certainly made mistakes in his interior and foreign strategies, displayed some weaknesses of behavior, and accumulated frustrations and conflicts, but he was also guided by an ideal: Congolese and African nationalism. Furthermore, he committed his life to the emancipation and prosperity of his nation.

Lumumba's critics and detractors often forget three facts. First, given the backgrounds of the leaders and the cultural and political contexts of colonization and emancipation, none of the nationalist Congolese discourses had developed to the fullest degree of sophistication. Second, Lumumba's term was extremely short (barely two months, and he spent most of that time away from the capital, on official missions or visits to hot spots), and was full of complex and unexpected crises. Third, the MNC had a detailed program, and both while Lumumba was campaigning and while he was in office, he argued that a political sovereignty not supported by economic emancipation and development could not survive. His ascent—and he did rise before he fell—relied on objective facts like these.

Some of Lumumba's tactical "errors" are questionable. Most authors remark on the same ones: the virulence of the Independence Day speech; his policies and actions in trying to solve the Congolese crisis; his nonconciliatory attitude toward the executives and representatives of the U.N., and the mere fact of resorting to U.N. intervention, on July 10, 1960; and the tragic expedition to South Kasai, resulting in a massacre of at least 300 Luba Kasai civilians, including women, children, and the old. He is also criticized for lacking political foresight, sagacity, realism, and diplomacy; for blind ambition to the point of megalomania; for inflexibility; for ignoring the advice of counselors, friends, and protectors; for lack of control over his cabinet; for the utter and obvious powerlessness of his government to handle the national crisis; for his strategy of military occupation; for having no coherent system of planning; for the structure of his small cabinet, and for his choice of ministers; for naïveté, particularly in his patriotism and his sense of mission; for overconfidence—in his people, in his own efficiency, in nonviolence, in the supremacy of the law, in the magic power of oratory, and so on; for bad choices, notably in his leanings toward the Communists, in playing the Soviet card at a crucial moment of the cold war, and in the way he handled Mobutu's attempt to "neutralize" him and organized his escape to Stanleyville; and more.(fig. 37).

Mutatis mutandis, Lumumba was more the victim of the Western fear that he would jeopardize international interests than of these "errors." He was one of the first black African victims of international imperialism. His death became inevitable: "If Lumumba is in the way, Lumumba disappears," Fanon emphatically concludes (1967:196). Lumumba himself prophecied his own martyrdom in terms of shared responsibility (less internal than foreign): "If I die tomorrow, it will be because a foreigner has armed a Congolese" (McKown 1969:170).

One thing is sure: in 1960, Lumumba had more powerful enemies than committed and able friends. Among the former were important national and international pressure groups: a good portion of the Parliament; disappointed and frustrated clerks, soldiers, and other social and professional groups convinced that they were being "left out" in the postindependence share; theoretically privileged categories in both the executive and legislative branches, who felt threatened by the planned salary reform; the press; the unions; and the Church, which was frightened by Lumumba's liberal, secular, and "Communist" tendencies. In addition, Lumumba faced the coldness and even hostility of the population of the capital, the secessionist provinces, the moderate factions, and the West. He also failed to control the Congo's two most important political and economic poles, Léopoldville and Élisabethville. For Aimé Césaire, Lumumba was the first great victim of the cold war. For the saddened Fanon, his failure and death were predictable: in challenging the West and in compromising Western interests, this courageous leader had gone too far.

Lumumba's detractors accused him of every possible evil. His alleged vices, and those of the ethnic group that supported him, were said to include: atheism, anticlericalism, anticolonialism, racism, tribalism, ethnic exclusionism, Communism, arrogance, dictatorship, imperialism, ambition, Machiavellianism, insubordination, bellicosity, and extreme fanaticism around the figure of the "god," the "liberator," the Nkumekanga (the leader of an ethnic group). These charges appeared openly in a tract that circulated in the capital and the interior cities in July 1960, *"Draft That Every Ankutshu [Bakusu] Should Possess and Memorize* (Rouch 1961:35–36).

Lumumba the "Communist" or the "Nationalist": A Controversial Portrait

The accusations of Communism alone during Lumumba's trial deserve more than a short paragraph or even section. This is an obscure field in Lumumba's and the Congo's history, with rumors and elusive connections being mixed with real facts. In the postwar atmosphere, "Communism" was an easy, stereotypical slogan—no more than a synonym for nationalism and anticolonialism. Yet Lumumba himself never either confessed to Communist principles and methods or revealed that he had adopted them. He ruled the

Congo in a classic Western style, and always proclaimed the sacred Pan-African motto of "positive neutrality." In a press conference he delivered in New York on July 25, 1960, he even pretended to have no interest in "ideologies" or "blocs." And the political and economic structures of the Congo were inherited from the former colonial power.

Rumors of Lumumba's Communist sympathies included the negative campaign launched by the MNC leaders Kalonji and Nendaka, Lumumba's immediate enemies and rivals. Kalonji accused Lumumba of introducing "Communist methods" in his manner of ruling the party; Nendaka claimed that the Soviets had financed the MNC campaign by providing the funds to pay for twenty cars used in the elections. Certain questionable sources gave a precise amount: 10 million Belgian francs ($200,000), coming either directly from Moscow or through the Belgian Communist Party. Other rumors claimed the secret presence of Soviet agents and technicians in the Congo, both before and after June 1960; a conspiracy involving the Belgian Communist Party; the arrival of a Soviet plane at Léopoldville on July 7, 1960; the delivery of military equipment and cars from Moscow and Warsaw at Matadi; and the use of Soviet equipment, troops, and officers in the South Kasai foray. Some pointed to the people around Lumumba, most often mentioning Andrée Blouin, A. Djin, Serge Michel, Félix Moumié, Van Lierde, Diallo Telli, and others; the continuous assistance of Communist and Socialist nations; the attendance of Marxist-Leninist courses by Lumumba, Antoine Gizenga, and Anicet Kashamura; and the secret missions of Lumumbist leaders to Communist countries. In sum, Pierre Houart felt able to justify Lumumba's failure by "the Communist penetration in the Congo" (1961).

If the liberalism of Lumumba's thought is established, and was linked to his "godfather" Buisseret, his anticlericalism and atheism are uncertain and questionable. The latter is more easily explained by his frustrations within the missionary society in which he had grown up than as a loyalty to Marxist-Leninist ideology. Lumumba never declared himself atheist and anticlerical, but repeatedly proclaimed his Christian roots, faith, and practice. He was not at all discreet about his financial support of Christian organizations. As Benoît Verhaegen confirms, Lumumba's letter of January 4, 1961, to his intimate friend Albert Onawelo reveals the image of a deeply religious man (1978:87).

All this said, is it worthwhile and even possible to draw an objective portrait of this controversial personality? Some features emerge as accepted realities. Lumumba was a self-made leader. He did not enjoy the advantages of advanced or even regular schooling, or the support of the colonial church and administration. He was neither a former seminarian, teacher, or nurse, nor a classic clerk advancing through the stages of promotion. He did not begin his public activities in the capital. In Léopoldville, where the Tetela were a minority, he faced the hostility of the most important ethnic groups. Yet as a self-taught leader he showed obvious intellectual skills. He found it easy to make social, ethnic, and professional contacts. Although he came to a tragic end, he was a fine tactician who during his ascent skillfully handled the electorate, including all the Congolese and European ethnic groups. His party's rapid success demonstrates his managerial skills and political instinct. He was also an impressive orator, able to hypnotize, captivate, and conquer large crowds, to be "seductive" and "charming" and to develop a special physical and emotional rapport. He is said to have impressed those around him by his exceptional capacity for intellectual work. According to a certain reliable rumor, he owed his outstanding vitality and indeed his mere survival while in office to his nervous habits of drinking and of smoking hemp. Lumumba also had the reputation of a sociable man, full of gaiety and warmth (although he often succumbed to bad moods). He was a committed advocate of the people, and believed profoundly in the value of friendship. He had intimate European friends, including Pierre Clément (1960), Van Lierde (1961, 1963, 1972, 1988), and Luis Lopez Alvarez (1964). Lumumba almost revered his Pan-African "godfathers," especially Nkrumah.

Contrary to popular belief, Lumumba cultivated simplicity and humility more than even legitimate ambition and pride. Very early on, he was convinced of his mission in the Congo and in Africa generally, and he embraced his fate with an awareness of being a "hero," a "martyr" of both the Congolese and the African causes. "I am in a bad position," he told the journalist P. Scholl-Latour, while already under house arrest; "I will maybe have to die for the unity and the independence of my nation. I will maybe have to render a last and great service to the Congo by sacrificing my life. Africa needs martyrs." In his last conversation with the faithful minister Thomas Kanza, he seemed haunted by the same premonitory idea of death and sacrifice: "One of us [Kasa-Vubu or Lumumba] must sacrifice himself if the Congolese people are to understand and accept the ideal for which we are fighting. My death will hasten the Congo's liberation and will help us get rid of the imperialist and colonial yoke" (Willame 1990:437). Lumumba had a strong personality, and a keen sense of pride in his social, political, and intellectual successes. He was blindly committed to his ideals; his courage and determination pushed him irresistibly to the battlefield. Although he was an able tactician, he was naive and idealistic—deadly attributes for a leader.

From a negative perspective, Lumumba was seen as a demagogue (a charge Jules Chomé contradicts; 1961:42). He blew hot and cold, he was a hypocrite, all things to all men, opportunistic, egocentric, exhibitionistic, sensational, ambitious, greedy, haughty, overconfident, "highly excitable," unhealthy in his behavior, blinded by an "inflexible mind," in a "perpetual state of frenzy", etc. (Merriam 1961:287–97, Legum 1966:xxix). Between July 1960 and February 1961, the conservative Belgian daily newspaper *La Libre Belgique* called Lumumba a "cruel man," insane, incapable of ruling, a "rabble-rouser," a "crazy and criminal adventurer," a "sinister bandit," a "notable swindler," a "paranoiac" betrayed by his "feline mask," his "biting and mobile look," his "extreme agitation," his propensity to alcoholism and drugs, his "long arms," his "satanic goatee." He was considered the vehicle of a bellicose, savage ethnic ascendance. Curiously, the same newspaper had praised Lumumba some months earlier as an "orator," a leader with an "astonishing political flair," a "violent man who controls himself." In May and June of

FIG. 37.
Lumumba at Stanleyville (Kisangani).
By Burozi, signed Tshibumba Kanda M.
Oil on fabric, 16½ x 23 in.

1960, Lumumba still stood as an "able politician," an "ideal former" of the new government, a "man capable of imposing his policy."

Lumumba was a controversial personality, an enigma alternatively viewed as "god" and "devil" (Halen and Riesz 1997). "Strange Lumumba" to say the least (Kestergat 1986:7)!

Lumumba's Legacy in the Congo/Zaire

Right after the "official" announcement of Lumumba's death by the Katangese government, acts of violence were recorded in the Lumumbist fiefs, mainly in Stanleyville, Bukavu, Maniema, and Sankuru. The reprisals varied from minor humiliations, serious molestation, rapes, beatings, and expulsions of Europeans (few, however, were killed) to pillages and different forms of vandalism, "neutralization," ostracism, threats, and the execution of PNP men and other Congolese anti-Lumumbists.

On August 2, 1961, as a first sign of peace and national reconciliation, Cyrille Adoula formed a government of "national union." Among other Lumumbists, it included Gizenga, the former ruler of the Stanleyville regime. The continuing Lumumbist nightmare is rampant in the political chronology of the Congo from 1960 to the present, as evidenced in the monopolization of power by the notorious "Binza Group," headed by Mobutu. Whatever "liberator," "unifier," or "pacifier" was in office in Léopoldville/Kinshasa, Lumumbists were persecuted, excluded, prohibited, executed, and forced into exile. Reduced to covert activities, they attempted a first *coup de force* between 1963 and 1965; led by Pierre Mulele (formerly Lumumba's minister of education), Gaston Soumialot, Christophe Gbenye, and others, and supported by the Soviet bloc and by most of the governments that had recognized the former Stanleyville government, they conquered over two-thirds of the national territory. Thanks to Belgium and the United States, however, their rebellions were cruelly crushed. Mulelism, the "revolutionary" movement of the Congolese "Second Independence," ended in what Jean-Claude Willame considers a *"jacquerie"* (1990:476). Mulele himself was summarily executed on October 2, 1968, only three days after General Mobutu's sensational masquerade of official "amnesty" had brought him back to Léopoldville.

The 1960s saw armed rebellions, clandestine activities, and disparate pockets of political exiles. In addition, some professionals and intellectuals—generally small groups of progressive college students, such as the former Union Générale des Étudiants Congolais (UGEC), which was nationalist and Marxist in reputation—identified themselves as "Lumumbist." Their influence, however, was limited by the "New Regime." Even fiefs once typically Lumumbist are no longer unanimously attached to the late leader. To my knowledge, the only faithful surviving Lumumbist nucleus is located in Sankuru and Maniema, and its loyalty is questionable (more ethnical, regional, and sentimental than ideological and political).

Mobutu hoped to reinforce his power by taking advantage of Lumumba's popularity and even charisma. On the sixth anniversary of national independence, he solemnly announced the rehabilitation of the late prime minister by proclaiming him a national hero and announcing the construction of a monument in his memory. Going farther in this masquerade, on the occasion of the first anniversary of his own advent to power, he offered to support the publication of a book on the hero's "last fifty days" (Heinz and Donnay 1969); he even encouraged investigation of the scene of Lumumba's murder, and promised to make the site a museum. A new banknote showing the martyr was issued. Streets, avenues, boulevards, stadiums, hospitals, schools, planes, boats—all were named after the hero. Paradoxically, in both his discourse and his policies, Mobutu followed the ideological, political, cultural, and economic paths traced by Lumumba—but without referring to their originator. His appropriation of Lumumba's ideas—including concepts of "authenticity," "authentic Zairian nationalism," total independence, and ideological neutrality (rejecting "right," "left," and even "middle")—reinforced Lumumba's political silencing. Among other nationalist efforts, Mobutu borrowed concepts of freedom and "African dignity" as an absolute priority. He pursued the demystification of the *"Noko"* (the uncles, that is the Belgians), the unconditional defense of national unity, the eradication of separatism in Katanga, and the "pacification" and "unification" of a sickly nation torn by "congolization" (total chaos). Lumumba too had espoused the assertion of African identity, cultural revolution, and mental decolonization, as reflected in the names of people and places, in administrative and political terminology, in clothing, and in linguistic patterns. He too had advocated the establishment of a secular state, and even the formation of a popular unified party (the Mouvement Populaire de la Révolution).

The new Lumumbist cult, however, soon became a comedy of bad taste. Both Lumumbism and Lumumbists were outlawed nationwide. The official calendar omitted all events honoring the late prime minister's memory. The anniversary of Lumumba's death, January 17, became an ordinary day (except among the UGEC and small groups in the Diaspora, especially in Belgium), commemorative activities being prohibited. The figure of Lumumba was not even associated with the "Martyrs of Independence Day," celebrated every January 4 (the date of riots in the capital in 1959). Apparently the victims of colonial repression in the Stanleyville riots of late October 1959—riots that Lumumba led—were not counted among the pious "martyrs of independence." In official celebrations, *"Indépendance Cha-Cha,"* a popular song by Joseph Kabasele (alias Kallé Jeef) dedicated to the heroic Congolese leaders of the Brussels Round Table, and citing Lumumba at the top of the list, was censored. G. Heinz and H. Donnay's book was seized by Mobutu's security as soon as it reached the Congo. No rigorous investigation of Lumumba's murder scene ever took place; the Lumumba museum became an abandoned dream; and the incomplete monument to Lumumba fell into ruin without ever receiving his statue. Instead, in 1989, a huge monument was erected in Kamanyola to honor the heroic officer Mobutu. No city (not even Lubumbashi, contrary to common African belief), no institution of higher education, no building, nor any national organization was named after the "national hero."

Through government censorship and cruel repression, Lumumba became taboo in all intellectual and cultural arenas. Extensive, rigorous studies of the MNC leader are rare among Zairian scholars, intellectuals, and activists; when they appeared, they were generally published abroad, and late. Available sources indicate only two recent books, by Manya K'Omalowete (1985) and Kapita Mulopo (1992). The early books by Kashamura (1966) and Kanza (1978) are comprehensive and apologetic autobiographies paying tribute to the charismatic leader. The late patriotic singer Kabasele is among the rare artists to have immortalized Lumumba, both nationally and in the African continent. As Charles K. Djungu-Simba (1997) points out, Lumumba is also remarkably absent from, or timidly evoked in, Congolese/Zairian literature.

In 1990 there was a wave of "democratization," and after April of that year, Lumumbist parties were allowed to function, along with other Zairian political organizations. But "Lumumbism," which in the early and mid-1960s had signified a precise ideology and action, became a confused and confusing concept, even a relatively empty one. It was no longer synonymous with (radical) nationalism. For thirty years, after all, Mobutu had imposed his own divine figure as the "savior," "pacifier," "supreme" and "enlightened guide," "helmsman," "founder president," and "magnanimous father" of the Congolese/Zairian nation. Through the policy or ideology of authenticity, the "official" synonym of nationalism had become Mobutism. In Mobutist Zaire, Lumumbism was an atrophied, fading political and ideological force, merely symbolic even for many of its believers. A good number of "Lumumbists" were simply "nationalists" by another name. An emptied revolutionary arm, Lumumbism was merely a confusing political logo for many Zairians, of all ages, ethnic groups, and regions with few exceptions.

Mobutist propaganda had made it an abused and exploited slogan. The variety of "Lumumbist" parties and leaders alone illustrates this confusion: some Lumumbists were members of the opposition to Mobutu (early Lumumbism meant *the* opposition, with a host of variations) while others overtly supported the incarnated Mobutist reaction named *"mouvance présidentielle."*

The Lumumbism claimed by the country's current leader, Laurent Désiré Kabila, is questionable, despite his eloquent gestures. Like Mobutu, Kabila honored the "national hero" in his first speech to the nation (June 30, 1997); he appointed Lumumba's daughter Juliana to his cabinet; and his single bill on the subject of homage to political leaders names only Lumumba, Mpolo, and Okito. Some of the population, however, has simply construed these deeds as strategies to establish Kabila's own popularity and legitimacy. The creation since 1997 of the Kinshasa-based Centre d'Étude Patrice Lumumba and Fondation Patrice Émery Lumumba are increasing the national visibility of Lumumba's legacy, but these institutions are far from reaching several of their primary goals, including the organization of the first national conference on Lumumba.

... And Elsewhere ...

In the first days after the news of Lumumba's assassination, outbreaks of violence were recorded all over the world. Demonstrations and acts of vandalism were directed against targets representing the "killers": U.N., U.S., and Belgian consulates and embassies in Athens, Bonn, Cairo, Caracas, Copenhagen, Dakar, Djakarta, Havana, Johannesburg, Lagos, Lima, London, Los Angeles, Montreal, New York, Paris, Prague, Singapore, Teheran, Tel Aviv, Tokyo, Warsaw, Washington, etc. A printing press and a locomotive in Accra, a public square in Beijing, a dance in Brazil, a sugar factory in Cuba, a theater and an African center in Paris, a factory and a college in the Soviet Union, a street and a bar in Warsaw, and so on, were named after Lumumba. Here and there commemorative stamps were issued in his honor. In Nigeria, the press praised him as "the Congolese hero," "a saint," even the "second God of the world." Records and plays were dedicated to the hero, whose grandeur was said to stand out from the frivolity, lack of discipline and responsibility, and "brawling character of his people." A columnist for *African Pilot* drew a parallel between Lumumba's and Christ's messianic destiny (in McKown 1969:187):

> Like the Christ of old, you came to your people, but your people knew you not. You redeemed them from slavery, but they turned around to betray you. On a platter of gold did you bring Independence to them, but they turned to make you a victim of Independence. You sought unity for your Congo, but they chose to sacrifice you on the altar of chaos.

The socialist regime of neighboring Congo Brazzaville, in celebrating the anniversary of Lumumba's death and valorizing him in books—such as Tchikaya U Tam'si's *Epitomé* (1962), Maxime N'Debeka's *Soleils neufs* (1969), and Sylvain Bemba's *Léopolis* (1984)—fostered the memory of the assassinated and outlawed son. In the Francophone world, the classic literary tribute to Lumumba is of course Césaire's *Une Saison au Congo* (1965). A recent film by Raoul Peck, *Lumumba: La Mort du prophète* (1992), narrates the Congolese leader's rise and fall. The Lumumba epic now covers dozens of books of various genres and tendencies in several languages.

The first notable victim of Western imperialism, Lumumba has entered the mythical tower of the "fathers of African independence." He is the precursor of a long list of African and Third World heroes and martyrs. While visiting a favela in Rio de Janeiro in 1987, the Congolese scholar and writer Lye Mudaba Yoka was pleasantly surprised and edified to discover images of Lumumba and Jesus next to each other on the altar of a sanctuary (in Kapita 1992:295–97). Early and recent writings, alternately apologetic and analytic, posit Lumumba as the "champion of African liberty" (Valodine 1961), the "archetype of the African nationalism" (Lopez Alvarez 1975), "the prophet of Negritude" (Sartre 1963), "un homme seul" (Van Lierde 1961:114), a "phenomenon" and a "meteor" (Van Lierde 1988). Others compare him to Savonarola (Willame 1990:7–9), Robespierre, Castro (Sartre 1963), etc. Jean-Paul Sartre (in Van Lierde 1963) also sees in Lumumba another Fanon, "a revolutionary without revolution," "not the hero, but the martyr of Pan-Africanism." Henceforth the sacrificed leader would incarnate the aspirations of a whole continent and race as the symbol of an "Africa always in search of new heroism" (Yoka, in Kapita 1992:297). Lumumba expresses "Congolese patriotism and African nationalism in their most rigorous and noblest sense" (Fanon 1967:193).

Lumumba, an "idea … "

Aware of the global consecration of Lumumba as the African hero, Lumumba's motherland is trying hard to recuperate the myth by identifying him with the history of the nation. In boasting the site of Lumumba's birth—his Bethlehem—the Congolese pretend to forget his Golgotha. Lumumba has become the "idea" he prophetically claimed to represent in his last days. In his testament *Letter to Pauline,* he writes, "Dead, living, free, or in prison … it is not I who counts[,] it is the Congo"; and "history will one day have its say" (in McKown 1969:175–77).

Needless to say, since January 1961, history has spoken, or at least stammered, even when intertwined with passions, manipulations, misconceptions, misinterpretations … and myths.

Popular Memories of Patrice Lumumba

Dibwe dia Mwembu

Can you imagine—someone who dared attack the Belgians publicly, insult them during the colonial period! You had to be Patrice Lumumba [to do that]. ... He woke up the Congolese, who had been plunged into the sleep of fear. So for the Belgians he was very dangerous.[1]

If "memory is a library" (Jewsiewicki 1987:4), it can also change with time: forgetting may set in and denature historical facts, confusing them with their larger context (figs. 39, 40). Memory can also be affected by the political situation of the moment, so that it no longer accurately reproduces recollections of the past. This is what has happened to the memory of Patrice Lumumba, which is both one and diverse, objective and subjective, depending on the recollecting individual, the period, and the interests and preoccupations of the moment. Most people of Katanga province, for example, remember and have an image of Lumumba today as either the liberator of the Congo or Katanga's sworn enemy.[2] Lumumba always impressed both adversaries and partisans with his courage and charisma. Not only did he know how to speak to crowds and stir them to action (sometimes even transforming them into fanatics), it is also believed that no one could stop him, or find arguments capable of invalidating his. The simple fact of having fought against the white man's power and won makes him into a kind of magician:

> Lumumba must have used fetish objects or black magic when he spoke, because no one could contradict him. When he called for the immediate independence of a united Congo, everyone was with him. Everyone applauded. ... When he finished his speech before the Belgians at the Round Table [talks] in Brussels (fig. 38),[3] no Belgian had the nerve to ask him questions or refute what he had said. The Belgians were truly afraid of Patrice Emery Lumumba.[4]

> When he spoke, the ground trembled, the radios jumped (fig. 40). The whites were ill at ease and couldn't sleep; they fled.[5]

For Lumumba, federalism was only a camouflage for tribalism and separatism; this made him the enemy of the Katangese federalists. As early as April 1960 an important functionary in the colonial administration wrote, "Monsieur Lumumba is considered by a great number of Katangese, both black and white, to be a kind of antechrist [sic]."[6] Shortly before the elections of May 1960, the Catholic Church threatened that any believer voting for "this communist, a friend of the Russians" would be excommunicated. Passou Lundula remembers being in the Saint Peter and Paul Cathedral of Lubumbashi when, as part of his homily, Monseigneur Floribert Cornelis addressed the congregation

FIG. 38.
Lumumba's Speech Causes Panic.
By Burozi. Oil on fabric, 15 x 19¼ in.

thus: "Who are you going to vote for? Not Lumumba—a communist who would like to see the Belgians leave and have the Russians replace them. Do you know what communism is? So you must vote for [Moïse] Tshombe, who wants to collaborate with the Belgians for the well-being of the Congolese."[7] Monseigneur Malula, bishop and future cardinal, expressed the same antipathy for Lumumba:

I make a solemn appeal to all who are proud of their traditional wealth and want to preserve it: repel atheist materialism as the prince of slaves, diametrically opposed to all the religious tendencies of the Bantu soul.[8]

Notwithstanding, the young Luba of northern Katanga praised Lumumba:

You the young, what do you want?
You the young, what do you want?
What do you want?
We want Lumumba.
He who is our savior,
The Savior of the Congo,
Who has saved us from Belgian slavery.[9]

Likewise the Songye[10] sang:

Monsieur Lumumba, Monsieur Lumumba, you, our strong man, Monsieur Lumumba, Monsieur Lumumba, you, our strong man, There are not two or three [of you]; you are alone, Lumumba. Monsieur Lumumba, Monsieur Lumumba, we support you, If not for you, we would not have escaped slavery. Monsieur Lumumba, Monsieur Lumumba, you, our strong man, You were sent by God to take us out from slavery (fig. 41). We are behind you, Monsieur Lumumba, Monsieur Lumumba, we fasten a belt around your hips and we support you, All that you are doing, that's what we want. We support you, Papa. It is you, Monsieur Lumumba, who will reunite the peoples.[11]

A few days after the Congo won independence, the country was shaken by military mutinies. On July 11, 1960, under the pretext of preventing the contagion from spreading to Katanga, Tshombe proclaimed independence for that province. Albert Kalonji of South Kasai followed suit, announcing the region's secession as an autonomous state on August 8 of that year.[12] To justify these secessions, Lumumba was portrayed as a communist who wanted to replace the Belgians with the Soviets. A public rumor accused him of having passed secret agreements with Moscow long before independence (see Brassinne and Kestergat 1991:153). Tshombe's agents said,

> Lumumba wanted to snatch our wealth for Léopoldville [Kinshasa]; he was a friend of the communists and he wanted to bring the Chinese and the Russians to the Congo. You know that the Russians had a very bad reputation in the Congo. They were bad people because of their communist system. That is, there would be no more private property. A wife would become everyone's wife, like a piece of common property, and so would the children, house, bicycle, and other objects. Everything would be held in common and belong to everyone. So you see, the people had to hold this against Lumumba and turn their back on him.[13]

Even the young Luba of northern Katanga, who had sung his praises, began to sing against him:

> Brothers and sisters, Lumumba has become a sadist,
> Brothers and sisters, Lumumba has become a sadist,
> Now he tells us he means to call in the Russians
> Now he tells us he means to call in the Russians,
> So that this land will become the land of the Russians,
> And we, we are calling Shabani to tell him
> That Lumumba has become a sadist.[14]

The Songye, on the other hand, who had never forgiven the Belgians for hanging their great chief Kamanda Ya Kaumbu in 1936, continued to encourage Lumumba; they were ready to accept the Russians if that was the only way to get rid of the Belgians. Opposed to an autonomous state of South Kasai, they believed that anyone who was against Lumumba was against the Songye:

We send out a ringing appeal to Monsieur Lumumba:

> If it doesn't work, call in the Russians
> So they may grab up this land and make it their own.
> We will die for the land of our ancestors
> And you, women, do not cry. Your lamentations discourage us.
> Monsieur Lumumba is with us,
> All the soldiers are behind him,
> He will rid us of slavery
> He is not doing this on his own; he is God's envoy.
> Friends, mothers, and fathers, we were deceived;
> Lumumba took us out of slavery in this year 1960.
> Even if we die, we die for our land.[15]

To stop the secessions, Lumumba sent the Congolese National Army (ANC) to Katanga, via Kasai. Led by Onombe, a Tetela like Lumumba, the army proceeded to massacre civilians in the town of Bakwanga (present-day Mbuji-Mayi). From then on, an important fraction of the Luba Kasai interpreted Lumumba's action as continuing that of Ngongo Leteta, who had enslaved their people earlier in the century. The following story is told:

> In the maternity hospital of Bonzola at Mbuji-Mayi, boy babies, considered potential enemies, were stabbed to death by Lumumba's military. The bellies of pregnant women were ripped open to find out the baby's sex. Lumumba behaved like Ngongo Leteta, who in his time ravaged the Luba Kasai population.[16]

At Lubumbashi (then called Elisabethville), in the camp, commonly known as the "Foire," where opponents of the Katanga secession had taken refuge, inhabitants of the Kasai region were split into two sides. The federalists, who supported Kalonji, blamed Lumumba for the ethnic conflicts in Katanga:

Kalonji, the bald man, strong and able to win the war against Lumumba,
who wants to sell off the Congo's land.
Wake up, brothers and sisters who have remained in Katanga,
Lumumba is going to massacre us like beasts.
If he shared Tshombe's opinion
We would not be suffering like this.
Brothers and sisters who have remained in Katanga,
Lumumba is going to massacre us like beasts.
If he shared Tshombe's opinion
We would not be suffering like this.
Brothers and sisters, wake up, we must not let our wives and children die.[17]

Lumumba's partisans, on the other hand, including the Songye, saw him as God's envoy:

Papa Lumumba, when you go forward, look behind you where children have
been left orphans.
Papa Lumumba [is] the man whose words are realized,
Papa Lumumba [is] the man who loves the people;
The people are reconverting.
Papa Lumumba, your birth is our joy, your death is our calamity.
We are behind you, you are the envoy of our God sent to take us out from slavery.
The white man came to draw borders and divide.
Papa Lumumba we are behind you.
Let us sing for Papa Lumumba,
Let us praise Papa Lumumba.[18]

The Luba of Katanga sang:

We are fighting for our land
We are fighting for this land bequeathed to us by our ancestors …
Lumumba and Sendwe[19] are the liberators of our country,
Lumumba and Sendwe are the liberators of our country.[20]

When Lumumba and two collaborators, Mpolo and Okito, were assassinated,[21] news
of their deaths was received with joy by Moïse Tshombe's influential minister, Godefroid
Munongo, who declared,

I would be lying if I said I was saddened by Lumumba's death. You know how
I feel about him: he is a common-law criminal who bears, among others, the
responsibility for thousands of deaths in Katanga and tens of thousands in
Kasai—and this is not counting the persecutions and exterminations in the
Province Orientale and Kivu.[22]

Yet at the "Foire" people sang farewell to the hero:

Lumumba, go in peace.
May our ancestors and our gods receive and keep you.
Go in peace, Savior of the Congo.[23]

For a long time the members of the MNC-L "did not believe that Lumumba could be
killed—especially if one remembered how his mere voice on the radio had sent the whites
into a panic. But as the days passed and we no longer heard his voice, we ultimately
came to believe that he was indeed dead. We lost a fine man."[24] Lumumba was believed
to have accepted death from the Belgian commandos in order to save his people:

"You are going to kill me—that's your problem," Lumumba is believed to have
said. "But before you do, let me tell you that you are all lazy people who don't
know how to reason. Do you think that by killing me the Congolese people are
going to turn back? You are fooling yourself to reason that way. I am going to

die—but for my people. I am proud of this. And now, what are you waiting for? Get it over with. I have no more time to lose."[25]

Over time, however, people became resigned: "People with good hearts do not live long. Jesus himself, who came to save the world, did not live long in this world."[26] Lumumba was thought to have sacrificed himself for the Congo's independence:

> [Refrain] Long live Lumumba's independent Congo
> He suffered————Lumumba
> For the Congo————Lumumba
> He was arrested————Lumumba
> For the Congo————Lumumba
> He was whipped————Lumumba
> For the Congo————Lumumba
> He died————Lumumba
> For the Congo————Lumumba
> Long live Lumumba's independent Congo
> Long live Lumumba's independent Congo.[27]

For some time his spirit was invoked in times of necessity, as when the Lumumbist rebels had to combat the Katangese "gendarmes" and later the Congolese regular army:

> We're calling you, Papa Lumumba,
> Come, come save us.
> The lion is roaring in our country,
> Our enemies are closer to us.
> Come from the beyond and cast out our enemies.[28]

But eventually other events began to hold people's attention. In January 1963, the Katangese secession was definitively quashed; Tshombe went into exile, then returned to lead the country in July 1964. Next came pacification, the rebels' military failure, and, on November 24, 1965, Joseph-Désiré Mobutu's coup d'état. Lumumba's partisans began their exile; the hero fell into disgrace; and little by little his memory faded.

In 1967, Mobutu turned the Congo into a single-party state. Many wondered then whether he wasn't trying to appropriate the cause of unitarist nationalism to legitimate his dictatorship (Kabuya-Lumuna Sando 1995:214). As early as 1966 he had proclaimed Lumumba a national hero, and Lumumba's image appeared on the 20-makuta banknote. Later Mobutu announced the construction of monuments in honor of three national heroes: his wife, Marie Antoinette, who had died a short time before; Lumumba; and Joseph Kasa-Vubu. Main avenues in the country's cities were also named after Lumumba. Even so, Mobutu quickly became the only figure that the people could legitimately revere. The 20-makuta banknote in Lumumba's image was replaced by a coin bearing Mobutu's face. The promised monuments were never built, and to keep an image of a bloodthirsty Lumumba in people's memories, Mobutu declared, "It's thanks to me that the Muluba people were spared extermination, because I disobeyed the orders of my superiors."[29] This allusion to the events of 1960 at Bakwanga came in response to popular pressure to explain the massacre of native diamond-craftsmen in eastern Kasai in 1979.

Against this propaganda, the Tetela lifted up the memory of the liberator of the Congo, the only true leopard.[30] They refused to concede this symbol of supreme power to Mobutu the dictator:

> Lumumba freed Zaire [Congo] from slavery,
> Where might I see him again?
> The dignitary, the Leopard!
> The dignitary, the Leopard!

Lumumba freed Zaire from slavery,
Where might I see him again?
Oh my grief!
Oh my grief![31]

Popular imagination came to be dominated by the comparison between Lumumba and Christ, a comparison that implicitly made it possible to exempt the Congolese from responsibility for his death:

> God has punished us. He is angry because the Belgians used us to assassinate Lumumba. The Jews preferred that Jesus Christ die in Barabas's place. The same is true for the Congolese. The Congolese preferred Mobutu instead of Lumumba and thereby sent Lumumba to his death. It was the Roman authorities who wanted to be through with Jesus. They pushed the Jews to choose to crucify Jesus and free Barabas. It's the same thing in Lumumba's case. The Belgians were against Lumumba; they incited the Congolese to kill Lumumba by bringing false accusations against him, as was the case for Jesus.[32]

It was not hard to move from such comparisons to worshipping Lumumba. He was said to have liberated the Congolese people from the colonial yoke just as Jesus had liberated the world from Satan's grip:

> Patrice Lumumba had the mission of leading the Congolese people to independence. Once this mission was accomplished, Lumumba died. Jesus Christ died at the end of his mission, which was to save mankind. If the people are still under the domination of sin and evil, this is because they don't want to practice the teachings of Jesus Christ. Likewise, if today the Congolese are sinking into miserable poverty, this is because they never put into practice the theories Lumumba developed (fig. 67).[33]

Christ died at the hands of his people; so did Lumumba. Christ died in the company of two evildoers; Lumumba, too, died in the presence of two of his collaborators (Mpolo and Okito). The similarities are so striking to many people that they believe Lumumba is not dead—that he will come back among his people one day, as Jesus did after his Resurrection.

At Kisangani, the Lumumbists' stronghold, there was a Kitawala church[34] in which Lumumba was adored as the black Christ (coming after the black John the Baptist, Simon Kimbangu):

> There was a secret Kitawala religious sect at Kisangani. During the 1960s Lumumba's extremely charismatic personality struck more than one person. His imprisonments and releases, and his sudden departure for the Round Table talks in Brussels, had astounded the illiterate population of Kisangani. The fact that after his meetings Lumumba went to the cemetery to pay homage to the deceased partisans of his party gave rise to rumors that the dead would come back to life on Independence Day. This idea already suggested that Lumumba was immortal.

> With the advent of independence, we witnessed the whites' departure in great numbers from Kisangani; they were fearful of the political climate that had taken over the place. The members of the Kitawala sect attributed this to Lumumba. But Lumumba's immortality was called into doubt seven months after independence, when people waiting for Prime Minister Lumumba to arrive at Kisangani learned the news of his assassination in Katanga. Then came the period of rebellion, during which the city of Kisangani went through indescribable massacres. It was a Kitawala sect follower who led those massacres, after declaring himself "first bourgmestre" of the city of Kisangani.[35] The Kitawala sect was legalized. The first bourgmestre had the Catholics persecuted and all the monuments to the saints destroyed. In September 1965 we watched as General Olenga and Sumialot, Defense Minister of

the rebel government, arrived at Kisangani. The slogan "Mulele mayi" was replaced with "Lumumba mayi" ["Lumumba the water"—a cry that makes the utterer immune to bullets]. But there was a conflict between the members of the rebel government and the Kitawala members led by the first bourgmestre. The bourgmestre proclaimed everywhere that he was the real power; that his mission was to prepare for the coming of Lumumba, who was not dead because he was invulnerable; and that all the Kitawala followers were likewise invulnerable. There was a power struggle between the army of General Olenga and the Kitawala followers. All the Kitawala followers, including their leader, the first bourgmestre, were killed in the first hail of bullets. It should be noted that among the dead followers was my maternal aunt's husband. She and many other followers are still waiting for the resurrection of their friends, their husbands … all dead; people who will be resuscitated and come back from the Lumumbist realm.

The Lumumba cult still exists. My paternal aunt still sets flowers and perfume before the effigy of Lumumba in her bedroom; the liberator is shown holding the globe of the earth in his hands. During the worship ceremony she wears a white robe and smokes cigarettes. When the worshipers of Lumumba get together for their ceremony, they intone the following hymn:

Many people believe that Lumumba is already dead,
Many people believe that Lumumba is already dead.
[Refrain] Love, oh! oh! Love oh! oh! Love.
The love of Papa Lumumba.[36]

The Lumumba cult practiced at Kisangani may have influenced the Songye, some of whom see Lumumba as the "Jesus" of the blacks. Followers of the Kabukulu Church (Church of the Ancestors) created by the inhabitants of the village of Kabungie, in the zone of Kabinda, also invoke the spirit of Lumumba, and consider all the martyrs of the struggle for independence to be saints who can intercede with God. They celebrate Christmas on June 30 of every year.[37]

Like Moses, Lumumba is believed incorruptible. The whites asked him to choose beween money and the bit of earth for which he was ready to die; he responded by acting like Moses, who preferred to serve God by sharing the destiny of his enslaved brethren rather than accept the life at court offered him by the pharaoh's daughter. This is how people interpret the image of Lumumba holding the globe in his hands.[38] The Congolese politicians are compared to the Israelites, who, in the middle of the desert, blamed Moses for taking them out of Egypt: many Congolese blamed Lumumba for liberating them from colonialism only to plunge them into Mobutuism. Moreover, just as Moses never lived in the promised land, so Lumumba never enjoyed the fruits of independence.[39]

In 1979, the Société des historiens zaïrois organised a colloquium on the history of Zaire entitled "Elites and the Future of Zairean Society." A paper delivered at the conference discussed Lumumba as a model to be followed by the political elite in order to transcend tribal and ethnic barriers (Banjikila 1980). The participants recommended revalorizing all individuals who had been active leaders in the construction and enlightenment of Zairean society, all who had contributed to its well-being (ibid.). This was a discreet appeal to restore and rehabilitate the memory of Lumumba.

Stifled by Mobutuism, the people had long kept memory of Lumumba under wraps. "We could not speak of Lumumba or quote him in popular songs, under pain of imprisonment," an old Songye explained.[40] In the 1980s, anyone who publicly evoked Lumumba's name or displayed a photograph or portrait of him in the front room was considered a communist. Paintings and portraits representing him, together with all MNC-L party insignia, were hidden away in bedrooms and suitcases until better days.

Those who feared official searches confided these articles to old women, said the attorney Mr. Mutamba; because such women were considered witches, no one dared enter their bedrooms. People also hid their ties and suit jackets, which Mobutu had ordered them to replace with "abascosts"—collarless jackets such as he himself wore. The president even ordered military guards to prohibit access to the Brouwers house, already in ruins, where Lumumba and his two collaborators had been led after they arrived in Lubumbashi. The Lumumbists could no longer lay flowers there every January 17.[41]

Mobutu created the second "Independent State of the Congo." (The first, under the Belgian King Léopold II, had lasted from 1885 to 1908); Mobutuists made Mobutu into the second sovereign—a black Léopold II. Memory of Lumumba, though stifled by the rise of Mobutu, smoldered under the ashes, but the fact that Mobutu had been Lumumba's personal secretary, that he, like Lumumba, supported unitarist nationalism (or said he did), and that the evidence of his appallingly poor management of the res publica was overwhelming for more than a quarter of a century, actually worked to tarnish Lumumba's memory. Lumumba was threatened with a second political death.

Fig. 41.
Lumumba's public address. By Burozi, signed Tshibumba. Oil on fabric, 17¼ c 10 in.

In 1990, although Mobutu remained president, his dictatorship came to an end. People could now speak freely. Lumumba's name and images resurfaced in political life, together with suits and ties for men. The resurgence of the debate between unitarist and federalist nationalists directly affected memory of Lumumba. Etienne Tshisekedi, the leader of the radical opposition to Mobutu, was presented as continuing Lumumba's work. The Songye, meanwhile, saw Tshisekedi as no more than Albert Kalonji's former collaborator, appropriating the hero in order to win Songye, Tetela, and Kanyoka votes.[42]

On the national scene, at Kinshasa, Lumumba became the nationalist reference, the epitome of the selfless politician devoted to the people. One might even read the following editorial in a Mobutist weekly in October 1990:

Lumumba was a sincere nationalist—and a very popular politician into the bargain. Despite the campaign of falsehoods against his person and policies orchestrated and led by political adversaries and Western powers, and despite the fact that he is dead—assassinated—Lumumba has become indestructible. He has become an ideal.[43]

Christophe Gbenye, Lumumba's former minister and national president of the MNC-L, took on the task of proving that Lumumba had never been a communist:

When, as Prime Minister, Lumumba left on an official trip to the U.S.A. immediately after independence, Madame Bloin, a Guinean of mixed blood and the heeded advisor to a brother party, set about getting the Soviet Ambassador's help in bringing Lumumba down because he wasn't a real communist. The USSR said they would require the support of Guinean soldiers operating as part of the UN force in the Congo. The Guinean commander of these troops was himself a politician, an MP and member of the Party's Central Committee, dressed up as a military major. He told me and the others about the conspiracy against Lumumba. We begged him not to carry out the plan. And the conspiracy was foiled. When Lumumba returned and was told of it, he transferred Madame Bloin, then working in the office of the Council vice-president, to my Ministry to keep her under close surveillance. So Lumumba and his party were never in the communists' good graces (Gbenye 1990:27–28).

Gbenye also sought to show that it was Mobutu who was responsible for the 1960 massacre of civilians at Bakwanga:

It was on Kalonji's order that the Baluba rose up against the soldiers of the ANC [Congolese National Army], on their way to Katanga. Without any order or statement from the civil authority—which was myself at the time, as I occupied the positions of minister of the defense and the interior—and disregarding the military principle prohibiting combat against civilians, Colonel Mobutu ordered the massacre of August 27, 1960. And the Baluba were systematically decimated. … Let our compatriots understand once and for all: Lumumba, ever conciliatory toward human beings and nature, never carried within him the instinct of destruction (ibid:8–9).

In Katanga the 1990s have been marked by an increase in violence between Katangese of local origin and those originally from Kasai. We have seen the massive exclusion, even expulsion, of Kasaians, and the rejection of anything that evokes Kasai. Lumumba himself, as a Tetela, is taken for a Kasaian. The Katangese have sought to exonerate themselves of responsibility for the miserable poverty that has fallen on the country and the region since 1970. By killing Lumumba to keep Katanga independent, did they not prevent the true decolonization of the country? And in the transition period, did not their leader Nguz Karl I Bond not abandon the opposition and join forces with Mobutu? This is the feeling that pervades a letter from the Katanga bishops to Mobutu in 1993: "Already Lumumba's death has done great harm to Katanga in the eyes of the world. Still today people want to make the Katangese community bear the dreadful responsibility for, on the one hand, blocking the democratization process in Zaire and on the other, being a seat of tribal hatred."[44] On January 17, 1995, the thirty-fifth anniversary of Lumumba's assassination, the newspaper *Mzalendo*, published in Swahili at Lubumbashi, made the point that since Lumumba's death the country had not gotten back on its feet.[45]

The members of the Union of Independent Federalists and Republicans, Nguz Karl I Bond's party, whose slogan is "Katanga for the Katangese," have accused foreigners, namely the Kasaians, of pillaging Katanga's wealth. They say Congolese politicians are killing each other in the hope of getting their hands on the riches of Katanga, and that Lumumba was no different:

What attracted everybody was the Katanga province's overflowing wealth. Everyone wanted to get their hands on Katanga to get more of that wealth for himself. At first there were only two combatants against Moïse Tshombe, who was a barrier preventing them from pillaging the wealth of Katanga. As they struggled, Joseph Kasa-Vubu realized that his Prime Minister Lumumba, more alert than he, might well supplant him and be the only one to profit from Katanga's riches. So he began looking for an opportunity to take Lumumba out of the competition.[46]

The belief is also expressed that Katanga was not able to emancipate itself because Lumumba called in the United Nations to put down the secession:

> In leading the Congo to independence Lumumba went too fast. The Katangese already sensed this danger. They opted for a more effective system: federalism. All positions of responsibility should have gone to Katangese. But Lumumba used all his madness to divide the Katangese and make federalism fail. If Lumumba were still alive, I assure you the situation would be worse than it is today. I thank God for having rid us of that devil, who divided the Katangese. In killing each other we sacrificed our whole future. The unitarism that Lumumba called for has had only disastrous consequences for the Zaireans, especially for our province. We were not allowed to manage our wealth. Unitarism consisted only in pillaging our wealth. And Lumumba's diabolical spirit continues to act in the person of Mobutu, his former personal secretary. You know, I have a house I rent out. One day I met with a person who wanted to rent the house. The man wore his hair like Lumumba did, with the same part. And he wore glasses like Lumumba's. He also did his beard the same way. I sent him away. That man adored the devil; he was very dangerous.[47]

For the unitarists, "federalism is secessionist madness, it is civil war and colonialism, for which the selfish Katangese are responsible; it is putting Lumumba to a second death."[48] The persistance of unitarism ensures Lumumba's political survival. But on the opposite side of the political spectrum, the Katangese media has called the legitimacy of Lumumba's popularity into question, as in the following editorial in L'Eveil du Katanga:

> Tshombe owed his popularity to the real practice [of power] during the exercise of his functions as prime minister and afterward. Lumumba's case, for example, is quite different. Lumumba conquered his popularity before June 30, 1960, through the hope people placed in him, and despite or because of Westerners' hatred of him. This popularity grew enormously after Lumumba's death and because of his death, premature and brutal, a death snatched up by the Westerners' media in the service of a cause, their cause. … Lumumba's popularity thus appears to have been forged after the fact, for the medias—it is media popularity, mythical popularity. The grave made Lumumba. As it may do the same for Tshisekedi, for example. Indeed, a stray bullet would suffice these days to make Tshisekedi into another Lumumba, to win him popularity he doesn't have now, popularity that he doesn't deserve, that would not be owing to any governmental action, however positive. Like Lumumba, Tshisekedi represents (has represented) hope, a hope that the national and international media, the tribal and religious media, pound into the minds of our good people with editorials, interviews, news reports, homilies.[49]

Meanwhile, various strands of regional and ethnic Congolese memory try to appropriate Lumumba to themselves. The Songye present Lumumba as the legitimate successor of their great chief Kamanda Ya Kaumbu,[50] believed to have died for the cause of independence:

> The Songye state was led by great chiefs. As I just told you, in 1936 Chief Kamanda was arrested and hanged. The cause of Kamanda's death is still unknown to most people. It is generally known to the whites but only a few blacks know it. Kamanda had a white son-in-law, director of the Interfina at Kabinda.[51] He answered to the name of Monsieur Jacob and was a Belgian subject. Kamanda was educated; he spoke French correctly. He had studied here in Katanga, at Kafubu. He studied with chief Boniface Kabongo. All the children of great chiefs were brought here to Katanga to study under the Catholic missionaries.
>
> When his father Lumpungu-a-Kikola died, Kamanda was deemed fit to replace him. He was a celebrated, brave chief. He feared no one. During Kamanda's reign, Jacob married his daughter. One day Jacob said to his father-in-law: "You have let the years for becoming independent go by. You are still colonized by us, the

Belgians. Colonization has a beginning and an end; the period of colonization is clearly determined. I propose to you the following: since you are a great chief, you must demand independence. You will be crowned like a king." Kamanda wrote a letter to the king of the Belgians demanding independence. Here is the substance of the letter: "To the king of Belgium. It is said in your law that a country must have its independence after 25 years. Thus and such country had its independence after so many years. Why, after that time limit, do we still not have our independence? Because of this, I, Chief Kamanda, demand that independence be granted to our country in a very short time." The letter was typed by Monsieur Jacob, his son-in-law. It was written in secret so that the whites in the place would not seize it. Chief Kamanda was unlike any chief living in a straw house. He lived in a multi-story house. He wore suits. My son, we had a chief who deserved the title. We lost someone who was someone!

The letter was sent and came into the hands of the king. After sending word that it had been received, the king and his subjects were very shocked. This was the atmosphere of tension that Kamanda created, as Monsieur Patrice Emery Lumumba would do later. … Kamanda died for having demanded independence from the king of the Belgians. To this day the people don't know that he was the first to demand independence (fig. 52).[52]

Certain Songye go so far in their admiration for Lumumba as to make the hero one of their own by having him descend from a Songye couple brought as slaves to the capital of Ngongo Leteta. They say the name "Lumumba" is of Songye origin, that it is actually Lumu Mbayu, which in the Tetela language has lost the final syllable "yu."[53]

Next to Mobutu, a Judas who betrayed Lumumba both physically and ideologically and who had had himself indiscriminately called "messiah, savior, enlightened guide, helmsman" with no justification; next to Tshisekedi, a tribal nationalist, Lumumba stands for the unitarists as the ideal politician, the providential man. God has not yet found a replacement for him to lead the people to prosperity. This is why Lumumba is not so much the Moses of the Congo as a Jesus. And it explains the cult worship of him.

1. Jean Mushidi, 60, retired mine worker for the Union Minière du Haut Katanga (UMHK), Katangese from Sandoa (Lunda ethnic group); interviewed in Lubumbashi, March 15 and 16, 1994.

2. Katanga province (now called Shaba), in southeastern Zaire (renamed Congo—or, in full, the Democratic Republic of Congo—when Laurent-Désiré Kabila took power in 1997), is a region rich in mineral reserves, namely copper, cobalt, uranium, and zinc. These minerals are the national "wealth" that is so often referred to in the press, and that the Belgians were so reluctant to lose.

3. The Round Table talks were the talks between the Belgian Parliament and Congolese leaders at which the terms for the Belgian Congo's independence were negotiated and set.

4. Raymond Nduba Kwebati, 75, retired mine worker for the UMHK, Katangese from Malemba Nkula (Luba Katanga ethnic group); interviewed at Lubumbashi, November 17, 1993.

5. Léon Tshilolo, 77, retired mine worker for the UMHK, Kasaian from Mbuji-Mayi (Luba Kasai ethnic group); interviewed at Lubumbashi, September 25, 1995.

6. A. Scholler, quoted by Kayamba Badye,1995–96, p.31.

7. Passou Lundula, Kasaian from Sankuru (Tetela ethnic group); interviewed at Lubumbashi on December 27, 1995. See also Lundula, *Lettre ouverte à Monseigneur Monsengwo* (Lubumbashi: Editions Passou, April 30, 1994), pp. 22–23.

8. Monseigneur Malula, quoted in Kabuya-Lumuna Sando, 1995, pp. 314–15.

9. Mwamba Kasongo, 63, Katangese from Bukama (Luba Katanga ethnic group), former Balubakat member; interviewed at Lubumbashi, November 9, 1995.

10 The Songye, an ethnic group from Kasai, are neighbors of the Tetela, Lumumba's group.

11. Kapenga, Kasaian from Kabinda (Songye ethnic group), former member of Lumumba's wing of the Mouvement National Congolais (MNC-L); interviewed at Kipushi, November 19, 1995. The words "We fasten a belt around your hips" mean "We support you 100 percent." Someone wearing a belt can at least be sure not to lose his pants.

12. The province of Kasai, in southern Zaire, is rich in diamond deposits.

13. Lwamba Bilonda, Northern Katanga, professor at the University of Lubumbashi; interviewed there, September 25, 1995.

14. Mwamba Kasongo (see note 9). Shabani was a local, village-level leader.

15. Kapenga (see note 11). According to Mr. Mutamba—an attorney, Kasaian from Kabinda (Songye ethnic group), interviewed at Lubumbashi, December 27, 1995—Lumumba wanted to convince the Songye chief Mutamba and the Songye to join him. In exchange, the Songye would be represented in the government, as in fact they were when Aloïs Kabangi joined the government.

16. Pierre Makuna, 67, Kasaian from Mbuji-Mayi (Luba Kasai ethnic group), political independent; interviewed at Lubumbashi, September 15, 1995.

17. Albert Lumpungu, 69, Kasaian from Bena Mpuka (Luba Kasai ethnic group), political independent; interviewed at Lubumbashi, September 14, 1995.

18. *Ibid*.

19. Sendwe was a Luba Katanga political leader.

20. Mwamba Kasongo (see note 9).

21. Captured in Mweka in the early hours of December 2, 1960, Lumumba was flown to Léopoldville (Kinshasa) and detained, first there, then in an army camp in Thysville. On January 17, 1961, Lumumba, Mpolo, and Okito were flown to Elisabethville (present-day Lubumbashi), where they were assassinated.

22. Godefroid Munongo, quoted in Brassinne and Kestergat, p. 190.

23. Mwamba Kasongo (see note 9).

24. Mukendi, 77, Kasaian from Bena Mpuka (Luba Kasai ethnic group), without political affiliation in 1970; interviewed at Lubumbashi, October 10, 1995.

25. Lumumba, as quoted by Mushidi (see note 1).

26. Mme Mwadi Mukali, 58, Kasaian from Mwene Ditu (Kanyoka ethnic group); interviewed at Lubumbashi, October 17, 1995.

27. Lwamba Bilonda (see note 3).

28. Mwamba Kasongo (see note 9).

29. Joseph–Désiré Mobutu, quoted in Kabeya-Lumuna Sando, 1995, p. 433.

30. When Mobutu appeared in public, he always wore a leopard-skin toque as a symbol of his strength.

31. Words quoted by Mme. Osako, Kasaian from Sankuru (Tetela ethnic group), assistant professor at the University of Lumumbashi; interviewed there September 26, 1995.

32. Léon Tshilolo (see note 51.).

33. Clément Badibanga, 63, farmer, Kasaian from Bakwa Kalonji (Luba Kasai ethnic group); interviewed at Lumumbashi, September 30, 1995.

34. The Kitawala was a local church derived from the Jehovah's Witnesses.

35. "Bourgmestre" was the Belgian term for "mayor."

36. Isaac Bokongoli, 46, from Upper Zaire (Lokole ethnic group), graduate student in medicine; interviewed in Lubumbashi, October 28, 1995.

37. Shimata; interviewed at Lubumbashi, November 14, 1995.

38. Louis Ngongo, 75, from Lubao (Songye ethnic group); interviewed at Lubumbashi, March 20, 1994. Some Songye say that the fact that Lumumba is holding the globe in his hands simply signifies that he will ultimately dominate the world. This may be due to the influence of the Kitawala church, which affirms that a day will come when blacks will dominate whites.

39. Kitengie Nsumbu, 54, Kasaian from Lubao (Songye ethnic group); interviewed at Lubumbashi, October 28, 1995.

40. Interviewed in Lubumbashi, September 20, 1995.

41. Mutamba (see note 15).

42. Kitengie Nsumbu (see note 39).

43. *Salongo Sélection* 34 (October 25–31, 1990).

44. Letter from the Katanga bishops, published in the newspaper *Umoja,* May 10, 1993.

45. *Mzalendo,* special edition of January 17, 1995.

46. Patrice Mwansa, 65, tailor, from Kasenga (Bemba ethnic group); interviewed at Lubumbashi, January 17, 1994. Raphaël Makombo, 89; interviewed at Lubumbashi, September 3, 1993, made similar remarks.

47. Gabriel Kapend Tshikez, 60, Katangese from Kapanga (Lunda ethnic group); interviewed at Lubumbashi, October 19, 1995.

48. *L'Eveil du Katanga* 7 (November 1994).

49. *L'Eveil du Katanga* 11 (April 14, 1995).

50. This chief also had the title Lumpungu II (see Jewsiewicki, this catalogue).

51. Interfina was a Belgian commercial firm.

52. Benoît Kasatuka, 81, Kasaian from Kabinda (Songye ethnic group), former president of the MNC-L for the town of Jadotville (now Likasi) from 1960 to 1962; interviewed at Lubumbashi, June 15, 1993.

53. Ibid. Kibambe kia-Nkima (Songye ethnic group), an assistant professor at the University of Lumumbashi interviewed at Lubumbashi on December 22, 1995, also affirmed that Lumumba had Songye blood in his veins.

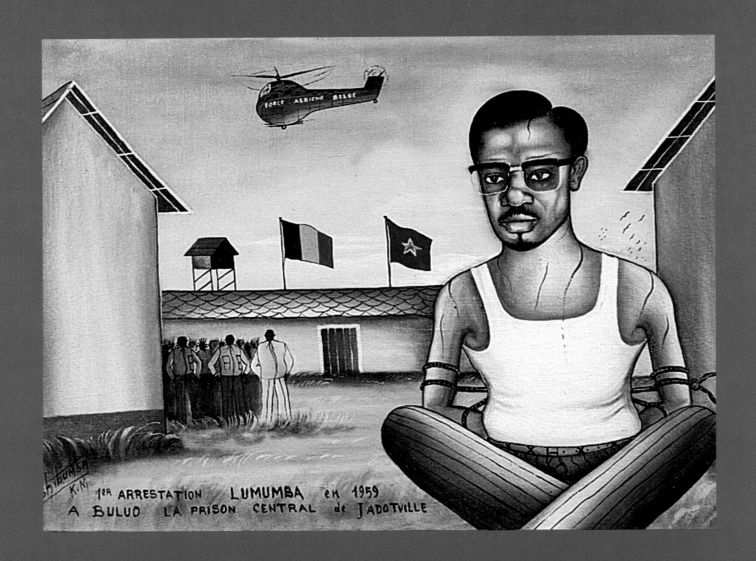

Congolese Memories of Lumumba: Between Cultural Hero and Humanity's Redeemer

Bogumil Jewsiewicki

Heroes are made to be reinvented—a different way each time [Glissant 1993:121].

Comparing Lumumba as historical personage with Lumumba as he appears in popular memory enables us to see how images of collective memory are constructed. Congolese popular paintings project aspects of the collective representation the Congolese have of themselves as a people demanding universal recognition of their dignity. They sketch a polis that has never yet come to be, a polis governed by equity and a sense of responsibility. The small number of icons to which the painters of these works have given shape are sustained by two types of memory, oral and pictorial. Both are resolutely modern, for the first type is postscriptural and the second postphotographic. And where they come together we see the contours of a representation of the political made up of three symbolic poles: Lumumba as cultural hero, Lumumba as Moses, and Lumumba as Jesus Christ. The aesthetic quality of these incarnations communicates to the viewer a virtual experience of a just world; the works make him or her feel as a tangible presence the political values to which the Congolese aspire. The artist, who enables us to see the icons by painting them, lives in close union with the memory that constitutes his material. In the paintings of popular artists, the viewer sees his or her own ethical values, the highest truth of his or her being, brought to collective consciousness. And the artwork is the common space in which all come together to debate about the world and with each other (Agamben 1996:61).

In each remembering community's representations of the hero we can read the "life story" of that community. Every image of Lumumba is a link attaching the past to the future, initiating an aesthetic discourse on ethical values and a political discourse on equity. Lumumba is a "realm of memory" (Nora 1998) in which people's multiple gazes on a historical figure, a landscape, an event, meet and confront each other. Lumumba neither lies nor speaks the truth; rather he makes a sign to us, an appeal from the depths of his time, time that has become eternity.

"Once upon a time there was a man." Because Lumumba was a man, his historical existence requires narration; no longer a man, he is himself a realm where memory labors and constructs stories to be told about the past that have meaning for the present. Downstream, the heroicizing of Lumumba makes use of tradition, whether oral or written, whereas upstream it provides a glimpse of a future that opens out onto the universal. In this aim it appropriates and makes use of Christianity. The heroicized personage slips the grip of time, but memory of him makes the work of time visible, thus enabling people to get a grip on him. The hero is constructed in such a way that he may escape death, but because he is not a god, he makes us feel how time leaves its mark on all that is human.

FIG. 42.
1er arrestation, Lumumba en 1959, à Buluo la Prison Central de Jadotville [1st Arrest, Lumumba in 1959 at Buluo Central Prison at Jadotville). By Tshibumba, K.M. Oil on fabric, 14¼ x 22 in.

A Cultural Hero and His Ancestors from the Colonial Past

Lumumba the assassination victim is a media personage belonging to the world of the second half of the twentieth century. As such, representation of him is not the exclusive property of his country of origin, much less his ethnic group or village. The circumstances of his political career, his death, and above all the political and ideological uses that have been made of him as a public personage have turned him into a universal hero. (fig. 43) Congolese social memory must reappropriate that hero. The Congolese had been attentive students of missionaries, who envisioned them as a great Christian tribe and sought to transform them into one (Kalulambi 1996). (In Kasai in the early twentieth century, in fact, the missionaries called them the "Bena Christo," attempting a mix of local and Christian culture.) If Lumumba's death left no body, then, that death for Congolese evokes the death of Christ.

From 1959 to 1961, Lumumba's public life provided these same missionaries with material from which to make a figure of the devil. Represented as the evil of Communism incarnate, he was a devil in which the Western right-wing political imagination was more than ready to believe. Lumumba was black, tall, thin, narrow faced, and wore a goatee. It was easy to bring him to life as the devil of Western fantasies—fantasies bloated with racism.

For the other side, the figure was already universal: he was the symbol of a state—a nation, even—that had been torn away from the Belgians. Carried off in the antiimperialist whirlwind, Lumumba in 1961 was already a symbol, an international ideological artifact. For many Congolese of the time, he was actually no more than snatches of a speech heard on the radio and retransmitted by word of mouth, an echo of words that had made the Belgians tremble, a memory of some fragment of a press photo or a face glimpsed during an election-campaign meeting. Appropriated by the world but also made greater by this passage through the universal imagination, the Lumumba of the Congolese people has had to search long and hard for a body that could become a Congolese realm of memory.

FIG. 43.
La rebellion au Congo. [The Congo rebellion].
By Tshibumba, K.M., 1975.
Oil on fabric, 15 x 24 in. Collection of James Bullard, Westport, NY.

Fig. 44.
Ngongo Lutete. By Mutanda wa Mutanda.
Oil on fabric, 12 x 23½ in.

The void left by a period of mourning that could have no end—because there was no body to bury—was gradually filled with images. If we compare the narratives gathered at Lubumbashi (see Dibwe dia Mwembu's essay in this catalogue) with popular paintings, we see that the images were painted with both a brush and living words. In them aesthetics become indistinguishable from political ethics. The beautiful is to be valued because of its political or social relevance; meanwhile the image can only touch its viewers if the particular aesthetics of the paintings enlighten them. Here, memory of the hero condemned by his executioners to eternal wandering encounters the idea of the Christian redeemer of all humanity. Christ was to be Lumumba's destiny, the memorial script of his life. The destruction of Lumumba's biological body was meant to tear him from the world and make him a nonbeing; instead, as we shall see, it has strengthened the aesthetic and political power of his image as Christ.

Regional memories have labored separately yet together on this universal realm of memory born of the Congolese earth, this realm of a return still expected and awaited. Like the rainbow in Luba-Lunda popular imagination, like the Holy Trinity, memory of Lumumba is a single whole composed of multiple, distinct parts.

The Tetela Warrior Ngongo Leteta and Lumumba the Warrior Leader

Lumumba as historical personage has not been approached and constructed in the same way by every strand of memory; the political figure is remembered in many different keys and tones. Even in the Sankuru region, where he was born, Lumumba is not a hero for everyone. The circumstances of his political activity, together with his political clumsiness and mistakes, have made it possible for some Tetela to construct a villain. His political conflicts with important Tetela chiefs; the violence practiced by his political party, the Mouvement National Congolais-Lumumba (MNC-L), against those chiefs, men who had been recognized by the colonial administration; and the memory of his impudent behavior toward his teachers when he was a schoolboy have made it possible for the Tetela to associate memory of Lumumba with memory of the leaders of armed gangs at the end of the nineteenth century. And as far as local politics are concerned, Lumumba as a public personality was swallowed up in the split between two factions of the Tetela ethnic group, the Ekonda and the Eswe.

Things become more problematic still when the figure of Lumumba comes into contact with conflicting ethnic memories of the Tetela chief Ngongo Leteta. Lumumba too was of Tetela ethnic origin, and though the ethnic basis for the association between the two figures is secondary, it is accredited by history. In the memory of the colonized people, Ngongo was the reverse image of the Western, Christian colonizer presented to them in colonial history schoolbooks: Ngongo was a cannibal. During the initial phase of colonial expansion, an effective alliance developed between the Belgians and the Luba Kasai, because the Luba were regularly attacked and raided by their neighbors and the local allies of those neighbors, among them Ngongo Leteta. Meanwhile, Luba memory was drinking in Belgian schoolbook history, in which the Belgians' antislavery crusade was presented in justification of the colonial state. An image of Ngongo Leteta cutting off heads and feeding on human flesh (fig. 44) was imagined as the pedestal for a monument to the colonial enterprise: this was supposed to be the life to which Belgian colonization had put an end. (It should be noted that as the Satan of the colonial imagination, Ngongo was thus universalized before any Congolese saint.) On the other side, in urban Katangese memory, Ngongo was interpreted and presented as a bastion of political opposition, a strong example of local tradition standing up to colonial modernity. Here the figure of Ngongo Leteta paved the way for a Christlike Lumumba—local modernity effacing colonial modernity.

Colonial schools never managed to eradicate the memory of the historical circumstances in which Ngongo was betrayed and put to death. He had become an official ally of the colonial administration, but was executed by the colonialists when he attempted to affirm his own sovereignty. Memory of Ngongo (like that of the Songye chief Lumpungu II, Kamanda ya Kaumbu) (fig. 46–51) resonates in Lumumba's celebrated speech of June 30, 1960. And it echoes in Tetela memory in the form of a question asked by important Tetela personages during one of Lumumba's visits to his native village: "Tasumbu [one of Lumumba's given names], do you believe that the whites are going to leave you in peace now that you've stripped them of all their authority?" (Mbuyamba 1997:134).

In Luba memory, especially that of the Luba of eastern Kasai, Lumumba is attributed the role of a bloodthirsty chief, calling to mind Ngongo Leteta or the Songye chief Lumpungu I. For them, Prime Minister Lumumba simply consolidated the colonial state's betrayal. On the eve of independence at Luluabourg (now Kananga), then the capital of Kasai Province, the Luba, educated people who had shown themselves to be hard and loyal workers, were abandoned by the provincial colonial administration in favor of the Lulua, peasants who had the advantage of being originally of the region. The result was a Luba exodus to eastern Kasai, which soon announced its secession from Lumumba's central government. Shortly thereafter, in his role as defender of a unified Congo, Lumumba sent the Congolese National Army (ANC) to quash the Katanga and Kasai secessions. The army, following the ways of the colonial army from which it derived, proceeded to pillage and to execute people. Luba memory of the killings follows the biblical model of the Massacre of the Innocents:

> Lumumba sent in his military men
> Lumumba sent in his military men, telling them
> Go to Bakwanga and massacre the Baluba (Makolo 1997:312).

Lumumba as Herod, seeking to prevent the emergence of a Luba state, thus became closely associated in Luba Kasai memory with Ngongo Leteta.

As prime minister in 1960, Lumumba incarnated the exactions of unitarism as much as he did the national state. The rebellions in the central and eastern regions of the country claimed to be popular leftist revolts; it must be added that their supporters worked hard to extirpate any trace of Western presence, which they believed had involved Congolese politicans and educated blacks in a subversion of the dreams of the independence movement. At the same time as the rebels fought against the state that they believed had betrayed them, they spoke of Lumumba as their father (Omasombo 1993:137), and they killed in his name, often in the presence of his effigy (Nzunguba 1994). These massacres—not only of whites, but of blacks such as teachers and office clerks who were suspected of having worked with the former colonial order—began to look like a sacrifice that would reverse the order of the world and assign to whites the place historically occupied by the people they had colonized. The icon entitled "Belgian colony," which represents an official colonial whipping of a black prisoner, was modified for the occasion: Simba combatants (simba means "lion" in Swahili) in "traditional" warrior dress are seen killing missionaries—but also Congolese teachers and office workers. In a painting from this period by Tshibumba Kanda, Lumumba appears as both a cultural hero and a warrior king nourished with sacrificial blood. (Fig.43)

Lumumba, a Tetela Cultural Hero

In Tetela memory of Lumumba as their own cultural hero we can recognize elements of a portrait painted by Kalume at Kisangani (fig. 27), the former rebel capital. The painting shows Lumumba as simultaneously traditional chief and modern man. A painting by Tshibumba, The Arrest at Lodja (fig. 45), shows Lumumba on his attempted flight from Léopoldville (Kinshasa) to Stanleyville (Kisangani) after losing his prime ministership. In fact we see him giving himself up to the soldiers pursuing him, in order to free his son, who had stayed behind: Lumumba as model father. The attributes of a traditional chief in the portrait by Kalume also emphasize this particular quality—the chief as father of all. But it must be kept in mind that Lumumba was also a modern, elegant man (with "elegance" having particular connotations of social importance and power), and that as such he would be adored in certain local churches as the God of Love.

Jean Tshonda Omasombo (1993:128–31) has published a translation of a chant written by Okito Mukanga of the musical ensemble Londolo la Anamongo (Music, or Drums, of the Anamongo; Anamongo is another name for the Tetela), and recorded as a single in 1978. The chant, entitled "The Owners of Music," tells the story of three heroes. They may be the founders of the three lineages that make up the Tetela ethnic group, but it

FIG. 45.
Arrestation à Lodja. [Arrest at Lodja].
By Tshibumba Kanda-Matulu.
Oil on fabric, 15½ x 25½ in. Bol Collection.

ARRESTATION · A · LODJA

FIG. 46. (ABOVE, TOP TO BOTTOM)
En 1936 Mme. Kapinga quitte Lubumbashi vers Kabinda accompagnée de son fils. [In 1936, Mme. Kapinga left Lubumbashi for Kabinda accompanied by her son]. By Tshibumba, K.M. Oil on fabric, 15 x 23½ in. Vincke Collection.

FIG. 47.
A leur arrivée a Kabinda Mme. Kapinga et son fils se présent aux autorités. [At her arrival at Kabinda, Mme. Kapinga introduced herself to the authorities]. By Tshibumba, K.M. Oil on fabric, 15 x 23½ in. Vincke Collection.

FIG. 48.
Kapinga se présente chez Lumpungu a Mwaba wa Mitanta. [Kapinga introduced herself to Lumpungu a Mwaba wa Mitanta]. By Tshibumba, K.M. Oil on fabric, 15 x 23½ in. Vincke Collection.

is also possible to see the text as recounting three episodes in Lumumba's life. It begins with an exhortation:

Anamongo, dance this tam-tam [music], for it belongs to you. Anamongo, put on the loincloths, this is everyone's tam-tam. … What is like you, tam-tam of honor?

The first hero, designated as "white, black, white," has left for Lodja—where Lumumba was arrested before being taken to the military camp of Binza (Kinshasa), then under the command of another Tetela, Jean Tshatshi. The second hero has left for Kingabwa, the district of Kinshasa where Lumumba was first put in prison and where he later attained political greatness. Of the third hero the chant says, "Tell me how he loves me superbly, always the same … ," and then, "Someone will die." The last words of the song are "utterly finished," signifying the hero's end.

Tetela popular memory clings to traits in Lumumba that assimilate him to a cultural hero. His birth is believed to have been announced by extraordinary signs, which have been enumerated by Jean Tshonda Omasombo (see this catalogue) and may also be found in a narrative collected in Kinshasa in 1995 by Alphonse Mbuyamba (1997:129). Legend has it that Lumumba was invulnerable to bullets: at Elisabethville it required no less a man than Godefroy Munongo, a descendant of Msiri, king of the Bayeke, to finally stab him to death with a bayonet (De Vos 1961:189).

A Tetela academic who published an essay on the hero in 1985 tells the story of a bottle of pure water that Lumumba gave to his family, a bottle still in their keeping. Legend has it that as long as the water has not turned red, Lumumba is still alive, in hiding, preparing to take revenge on his enemies. Another Tetela narrative affirms that during a brief visit to his native village in 1960, as part of the election campaign, Lumumba predicted his own death to the assembled notables, including the fact that he would die in Katanga. This is cited to prove that he, like the Songye chief Lumpungu II, had the power to choose the time and place of his death. He could not have been put to death if he had not consented. A narrative from Lubumbashi, on the other hand, attributes that death—symbolically—to Belgian commandos.

Orally transmitted memory, especially Tetela memory, imagines Lumumba as a prodigy come out of nowhere, born of poor parents, in some versions of slaves. From a thousand ordeals he emerges victorious and great. The voices and paintbrushes of the once colonized people, and the traces of the colonialists' feather pens that remain in the archives, reveal to us a man of multiple attributes. To remember, one needs tradition as well as history, press photos as well as holy images, object-signs that historicize a personage (see Nooter and Roberts, this catalogue) but also mimetic resemblances. It is therefore not surprising that Lumumba should be both Christian and customary hero, father of all and Satan, native satrap and a man whose studied elegance attests to his urbanity.

Lumumba's Predecessors in Katangese Urban Memory

Songye memory celebrates Chief Lumpungu II, who died in 1936, and who is implicitly given as Lumumba's ancestor, if only in the spiritual sense. People cite the fact that both men formulated and issued demands for independence, and became martyrs because of those demands. Certain narratives establish a direct tie between the Songye chief and Lumumba; they say that both of Lumumba's parents were Songye slaves brought to live and serve among the Tetela. In the industrial cities of Katanga, the death sentence and execution of Lumpungu II have worked to construct a field of competing narratives and denunciations focused on both the Luba Kasai (a large ethnic group) and the whites. According to these narratives, Lumpungu II was executed after the disappearance of a certain Madame Kapinga, a young women presented as socially white, either because she was a mulatto or a white man's housekeeper. (The chief was convicted of killing Madame Kapinga and her child and of eating her flesh to strengthen his power.) In certain versions of the story, the Luba chief Kabongo created the lady by magic to bring about Lumpungu's

FIG. 49. (Below, Top to bottom)
Kapinga prise dans le piège du chef Lumpungu.
[Kapinga is caught in the trap for Chief Lumpungu]. By Tshibumba, K.M.
Oil on fabric, 15 x 23 1/2 in. Vincke Collection.

FIG. 50.
Arrestation Lumpungu le chef Basonge à Kabinda. [Arrest of Lumpungu, the Songye Chief in Kabinda]. By Tshibumba, K.M.
Oil on fabric, 15 1/4 x 23 3/4 in. Vincke Collection.

FIG. 51.
Tentative de révolte à Kabinda. [Attempted revolt in Kabinda]. By Tshibumba, K.M.
Oil on fabric, 15 1/4 x 23 1/4 in. Vincke Collection.

downfall. In the urban context, the different versions of this narrative are told in a joking, ribbing tone, in bars over a glass of beer. They function to contain competition between workers of Luba origin and those of Songye origin. The story, which is based on historical fact, contrasts the Songye's early modernity—they were already seasoned industrial laborers—with the Luba's witchcraft, characteristic of the backward village society beyond which they had not at that time progressed. The accusation of witchcraft also connotes that, culturally and socially, the Luba were not "civilized" people. (figs. 46–52).

In the 1930s, after a reorganization of the colonial administration, the Luba chief Kabongo and the Songye chief Lumpungu II, already competing with each other for regional dominance, found themselves in direct confrontation. Legend has it that Kabongo succeeded in drawing Lumpungu into an ambush, and that the whites were merely his instrument in this—that he was therefore stronger than they were. For the Songye, this injustice and the white man's inability or unwillingness to reveal Kabongo's plot are all the more insulting because a pagan-devised conspiracy brought down a modern chief, a man who already in the 1930s had a car and a multistory house, and who dressed in Western clothes. Tshibumba has painted Lumpungu's court on the model of the "Belgian colony"(fig. 48): Lumpungu occupies the white man's place and is dressed as a white man. When telling this story, the Songye acknowledge the Luba's skill in tricking and eliminating Lumpungu, but they affirm at the same time their own modernity in contrast to their opponents' witchcraft. In this way they draw a moral advantage from the events, while also affirming that their seniority as industrial laborers living in the work camps of the Union minière du Haut-Katanga entitles them to "historical" rights. What happened to Lumpungu made them collective victims of both the white man's injustice and Luba witchcraft; as such they have a right to reparation.

In some Songye narratives of the death of Lumpungu II, the conspiracy is explained by his request—written and delivered to the Belgian king—for his people's independence. In this version the Belgians are no longer the instruments of Luba witchcraft; rather, the Luba are reduced to instruments of colonial domination. This story, encountered especially in interviews about

FIG. 52.
Lumpungu pendu a Kabinda. [Hanging of Lumpungu in Kabinda]. By Tshibumba. Oil on fabric, 12⅛ x 15¼ in. Vincke Collection.

memory of Lumumba, again situates the confrontation in the domain of justice—international justice and Christian justice alike. A white man, sometimes identified as Lumpungu's son-in-law (see Dibwe, this catalogue), appalled and indignant at the injustices committed by the colonial administration, is said to have helped the black chief denounce to the Belgian king the local administration's refusal to grant independence to his people. Because of an earlier agreement, the Songye (in some versions the Songye have become blacks in general) had a right to independence after a certain, predetermined period of colonial domination. Lumpungu was thus merely demanding his due: self-government for the Songye, or for the Congo as a whole. According to this story, his letter to the king was intercepted and immediately destroyed by the local colonial administration, for public knowledge that the right to independence had been flouted might in itself have been enough to bring independence. We see how the story becomes powerful by attributing power to justice. Accused, with or without the connivance of Luba witchcraft, of a crime he never committed, Lumpungu is executed to hide the truth. Divulging that truth could have the effect of reinstating justice. At the beginning of his early career as a colonial agent, Lumumba too seems to have believed that to denounce injustice was enough to rectify it.

It is impossible to say when these narratives first appeared, but we can see the relevance of the arguments they advance. Guided by a just white man, Lumpungu runs up against the local administration, which tries to stifle his demand for justice—a demand that might well be recognized by the distant Belgian king. This was precisely Lumumba's strategy between 1956 and 1959, when he appealed directly to the Belgian colonial minister and the king. A kinship between Lumumba and Lumpungu has also been established by ethnicity—by the relatively recent (and probably unfounded) claim that Lumumba's father was a slave of Songye origin, an origin here defined by place of birth, not, as is customary, by the origin of dowry property and other matrimonial rules. (This is the type of logic used by the Katangese, the "original inhabitants" of the region, who also demand a monopoly over their territory and all exploitation of its natural resources, and who prefer to exclude "foreigner.")

Several artists, in painting the scene of Lumpungu II's execution, have conferred a Christlike dimension on the Songye chief, who is believed to have died only at the moment he agreed to die to protect his people. Certain versions affirm that he refused to die far from his people, and that his execution could only be carried out once he had been brought back to his land at Kabinda. In all versions, Lumpungu three times transforms himself into a domestic animal (fig. 53), whose body replaces his own on the gal-

FIG. 53.
The miracle at the hanging of Lumpungu. By Tinda Lwimba. Oil on fabric, 15½ x 34½ in.

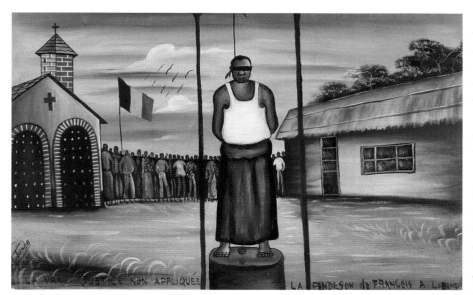

FIG. 54.
La vraie justice non appliquée, la pendeson de François à Lubumbashi. [True justice not applied. Hanging of François in Lumumbashi (Elisabethville). By Tshibumba. Oil on fabric, 15 x 24 in.

lows, preserving his life. It is only after the chief has demonstrated his powers, then, and only after explaining to his people that they must not exact vengeance because he is dying to save them, that he agrees to die. In the paintings, Lumpungu has been given certain features of the Songye Christ figure, just as many paintings present Lumumba as the Congolese Christ.

Finally, urban memory in Lubumbashi mentions another of Lumumba's "ancestors," who also demanded justice and tried to defend his dignity. Bwana François was a servant who caught his wife in adultery with his master. Having run for a knife to kill the man, he killed another white man by mistake, and, in 1922, was hanged in the public square of Elisabethville (Lumumbashi)—the last public execution in the Belgian Congo. In urban memory, the case of Bwana François (fig. 54) exemplifies the injustice of the colonial power. He too was a victim of the local administration, which prevented his request for a pardon from reaching Belgium, and even sped up the execution for fear that it might not take place at all (Vellut 1992). We cannot know for sure whether the Congolese ever knew this, but it is probable that they did. In any case, the spiritual similarity remains strong: Bwana François, like Lumpungu II and Lumumba, was a man brave enough to sacrifice his life in defense of his dignity.

The Flight out of Egypt: Lumumba Delivers His People from Colonial Slavery

A Tetela song, probably composed in 1959, affirms, *"Lumumba ambutshungula Congo umalu lohombo"* (Lumumba delivered the Congo out of slavery). On the 20-K banknote that Joseph-Désiré Mobutu put into circulation after proclaiming Lumumba a national hero on June 30, 1966, we see Lumumba leading his people out of the colonial era toward freedom (fig. 55). The chains of slavery are broken but have not yet fallen from his wrists. Certain popular paintings inspired by the image on the banknote celebrate Lumumba as an anti-Belgian nationalist, the elegant man of the speech of June 30, 1960, whose words broke the chains of colonial alienation—thereby breaking with history as a kind of curse closing off the Congolese future, just as Noah's curse closed down the future of his brother Shem.

FIG. 55.
Je veux que le peuple du Congo - soit libre. [I wish the people of the Congo to be free]. Probably by Abis. Oil on fabric, 19½ x 28 in.

This image celebrates not a radical Lumumba but rather the actual historical personage. The image of the liberator, the savior who restores to the Congolese people their humanity, is the same image that the schoolbooks in indigenous local languages had attributed to the white colonizer. In fact this image had been the pivot of colonial schoolbook history, around which all else turned, and it was probably what moved the young Lumumba to have himself called Patrice Osungu (Patrice the White). The "evolved" Lumumba of Stanleyville (Kisangani) presented himself to whites as well as to blacks as a protector of his people, a civilizing hero. This image of the liberator, who disciplines and purifies his body so that he may deserve to accede to civilization, belongs to a culture that substitutes the ancestors of Bena Christo, the Christian tribe of Congolese, for the Old Testament Hebrews (Kalulambi 1993). The black soldier with a whip in his hand is performing the task of purifying the body of the colonized people; this is the ritual by which the state is inscribed on the body of the subject. And yet, at least for the *"evolués,"* the ritual carried with it the promise of transfiguring an "ape"—the word expressed white contempt—into a civilized man of the just world. So it is that a former-colonial-administrator-turned-

FIG. 56.
Vive le 30 Juin 1960, Zaire Independence.
[Hurrah for Zaire Independence, 30 June 1960].
By Tshibumba. Oil on fabric, 15¼ x 25 in. Verbeek
Collection. Painting shows Lumumba signing
the Congolese Declaration of Independence in
the presence of Belgian King Baudouin.

novelist had his Congolese heroine (she is the mistress of a white man, and thus brings to mind Madame Kapinga) pronounce the following, virtually prophetic words:

> You sick people of June 30, the State ought never to have given us independence. The day the State abolished the whip last year—that was the end of Its authority for good and all! You'll see, the first thing Lumumba does will be to restore the lash (Geeraerts 1995:17).

In 1997, the new administration of the renascent Democratic Republic of the Congo did indeed reinstate public whippings, as punishment not only for infractions of rules and decrees but for the least offense against urban civility.

Lumumba, the Congolese Moses, restored the full rights of Congolese citizens within Christian historicity—that is one of the meanings of the June 30 speech. Pictorial memory presents him sitting before a great book set on a table, like Moses proclaiming the Ten Commandments to the people. In the memory of the colonized, the table and writing were the instruments by which they had come to be registered in the book of subjects—slaves—of the colonial state. But on June 30, 1960, thanks to Lumumba, those who had been slaves of the white man the day before—even though many of them were Christians—suddenly saw themselves proclaimed citizens of a sovereign state (fig. 56).

In their own subjective self-representation, most Congolese in the 1950s were a tribe—a flock—of God, aspiring to be led by their own shepherds. In 1959–60, some of them demanded the right to define themselves and be recognized as a sovereign people. They thus exchanged their ethical ground—ground already conceded to them by many colonial Belgians, including Placied Tempels—for political ground. To leave the land of Egypt, where tribes, clans, and families had suffered such a long period of slavery, first at the hands of Arab masters, then under the Belgians (in popular imagination all such masters are represented as white), was to be reborn. As a skillful politician, Lumumba was the midwife who would enable the "natives" raped by colonization to give birth to the collective Congolese "people" they carried in their belly.

According to the Biblical narrative, however, before God's people could reach the promised land, all Hebrews who were born slaves had to die. Isn't this also the first meaning behind Congolese memory's celebration of Lumumba as the prophet of his own death? The absence of a body makes continued hope conceivable: he will come back to complete his work—perhaps after forty years of mourning, when all those who were born slaves have died. Forty is also the number of days in the urban Congo between a death and the official end of mourning.

There is strong support for this Biblical metaphor in the actions of Lumumba the politician. As early as the 1940s, he knew how to exploit his relations with the whites to lift himself symbolically above the masses. As an adolescent in his village, he was already behaving like an "honorary" white man: "Patrice the White." Later, at Stanleyville, he managed to receive Minister of Colonies August Buisseret at his home, and to get an invitation to accompany the minister in his official car. The minister's agreement to share the private space of an *évolué,* who then paraded in public in his car—didn't that make Lumumba Pharaoh's vizier?(fig. 57). In popular representations of the earlier colonial period, the sedan chair *(tipoyi)* had been the very symbol of power. By the 1950s, the automobile had replaced the tipoyi as the sign of power, and to see a black man sharing it with a white man was to understand that the state could have a new owner (though this did not change the nature of the state). In the 1970s in Kinshasa, a Mercedes-Benz attested to its owner's place at the core of power; the children cried out *mundele* ("white" in Lingala) as it passed.

Not only did Lumumba obtain a seat in the *tipoyi;* he also spoke to King Baudouin during a royal visit to Kisangani, thus coming fully to deserve the name of Patrice Osungu. If we resituate Lumumba's book, *Le Congo terre d'avenir, est-il menacé?* (written in prison during his sentence for embezzlement), in this context, we see that it was neither treason nor, as political scientists like to say (Young 1994:258), a strategic gesture. (For a discussion of Lumumba's text see Rubango, this catalogue.) It was instead a way of consolidating an inheritance to come. Colonization presented itself as a mission conducted by people of a superior civilization seeking to elevate people of an inferior one. Lumumba-Moses was not a revolutionary; he was a perpetuator of the civilizing calling, and it is as such that he appears in the only representation that the autocrat Mobutu allowed there to be of him.

Tetela memory of a speech Lumumba gave in August or September of 1959 at the mission in Tshumbe clings to his promise of an escape from Egypt. A Tetela university professor named Manya (1985:31) "quotes" Lumumba from the memory of his informants: "The fundamental aim of the MNC is to liberate the Congolese people from the colonial regime." To deserve that liberation, the people had to demonstrate its own "unity." The future elites, whom Lumumba then called the "Congo of tomorrow," could not tolerate "a Congolese being identified with an ape or tortured with the whip." Further on, Manya writes, "Lumumba sought to deliver the Congolese people from their feelings of inferiority." In response to a question, Lumumba did not hesitate to evoke God's protection, and he closed the meeting to cries of *"Toyanga mimo lo lohombo l'asungu":* "We shall soon be free of the white man's slavery." A colonial functionary living in the region of Sankuru, witness

Fig. 58.
Lumumba, Master of the World.
By Burozi, signed Tshibumba, K.M.
Oil on fabric, 18 x 12½ in.

to one of Lumumba's political rallies on September 3, 1959, remembers that the French words *"esclavage"* and *"indépendance"* were used repeatedly (Extraits 1997:35).

At Stanleyville, Lumumba was living at the "court" of the whites who protected him: Pierre Clément, Buisseret, and others. He renounced personal advantage and came down to his people to help them pass through the barrier, the ocean, that separated them from *dipanda* (independence), freedom, and dignity. But the waters of the sea did not meet again after his symbolic passage of June 30, 1960: the hero had failed, at least for the time being. The hope so well expressed in Tshibumba's painting of the elegant Lumumba delivering the June 30 speech, his hand resting on a globe (figs. 58, 59), is underlined in a dialogue that Aimé Césaire (1993:23–24) attributes to a few ordinary citizens:

> *One citizen:* What is it exactly, your Dipenda? *Second citizen:* Idiot, it's a great big party! Our party. … It's when the Blacks command and the Whites obey! *A woman:* How does it come, Dipenda? By car, boat, airplane? *A man:* It comes with the little white king, Bwana Kitoko. [This was the nickname the people gave King Baudoin, young and elegantly dressed during his visit to the Belgian Congo.]

In 1989, in a song entitled "Analengo" (My brothers), the musician Shungu Wembadio—the internationally renowned Papa Wemba—proclaims, "The Atetela child is not a slave." Isn't this because that child is descended from Lumumba?

The Christlike Lumumba and the Move into the Political Sphere

In Katanga, urban memory seems to have gathered up into its bosom the figure of a Lumumba beached on the shore of millenarian hope. That memory has breathed new life into him, the life of the New Testament Christian ethos. Indeed the Lumumba who alternated between being an ancestor/cultural hero and an Old Testament Moses, he who neither lies nor speaks the truth but who makes a sign to us, has been reincarnated as a political symbol. Urban Katangese memory has developed a synthesis between the Old Testament, which Congolese Christian churches preferred to the New, and the epic narrative of origins specific to the political order. In this synthesis, the particular is no longer encompassed in the universal, as Western science would have it, but becomes instead the *source* of the universal. From now on (as a recent religious song from Kinshasa affirms), it doesn't matter whether Jesus was black or white; what counts is the certainty that he died to redeem me—a Congolese man or woman. We see that the way has been paved for a redeemer of humanity come forth from the *local* land.

Lumumba was in Katanga three times, the first in 1959, when he was imprisoned for six weeks at Bulolo (in Likasi, erstwhile Jadotville). He returned in 1959–60, for the electoral campaign, when he was a political ally of the Kasaians and of the Luba Katanga—all unitarists opposed to Moïse Tshombe's federalists. The third time he was taken to Katanga to be assassinated (on January 17, 1961). The painters clearly portray him as a victim of the secessionist Katangese government; they underline Belgian, American, and even United Nations complicity with the Katangese, and the secessionist state's unofficial alliances with these powers. Inscriptions on the paintings proclaim that Lumumba was martyred by imperialism and neocolonialism, and that he died for his people. The painters don't hesitate to accuse the Katangese in charge, including those who participated in the central Congolese government—though no one dared include the name of Mobutu, mentioning the real Judas only in private. Lumumba is celebrated as the martyr of *true* independence, the independence to which various rebels laid claim in the 1960s, not to mention, thirty years later, the army of Laurent Désiré Kabila, who deposed Mobutu in 1997. Lumumba's political party, the MNC-L, and Lumumba himself, the unitarist leader, were considered in Katanga to be "natural" associates of groups united by a common adversary. That adversary was Conakat, the political party of Tshombe, for it was Tshombe, the hero of Katangese identity, who planned and led the secession.

Indeed, it is between the two figures of Lumumba and Tshombe as they exist in Congolese memory, figures who could once again be discussed publicly in the 1990s, that Kabila has tried to insinuate himself in order to legitimate his proposal for a return to "the beginning"—the short-circuited independence of 1960. Kabila has proposed to bring about the rebirth of a modern country from the ashes of Mobutism. This country would take its inspiration from the urban industrial experience of Katanga. At the end of 1997, a rumor circulated (it was probably started by Kabila's propaganda service) that Kabila was to marry one of Lumumba's daughter's, Juliana. The image that Kabila, who is of Luba Katanga origin but born in the industrial city of Likasi, would like to project is that of a hunter come down from the mountain forests of northern Katanga, and who, like a contemporary Chibinda Ilunga (founder of the state, in the Luba and Lunda epic), would stretch out his hand to grasp the sacred bracelet of Lunda tradition—a bracelet in this case fastened around the wrist of Juliana, daughter of the nationalist hero Lumumba. (According to the epic, the bracelet of Princess Lueji was Chibinda Ilunga's source of political legitimacy; see Nooter and Roberts in this volume.) Himself a Lumumbist, Kabila would then be committing incest with his generational "daughter," because as Lumumba's companion—Lumumba himself acknowledged him as such—he belongs to the generation of the "fathers" of independence. Surviving incest is taken as proof that one has been elected by the ancients to the highest political position (for, having committed that sin, one must be exceptionally strong or blessed if one is not to be struck down); to possess the bracelet of power is to possess political legitimacy. This imaginary marriage sums up only too clearly Kabila's quest for legitimacy: it is expressed in the mode of the Luba and Lunda epic and alludes to memory of Tshombe (himself a Lunda), while the sacred bracelet is here a figure for Lumumba's Christlike martyrdom.

During the 1970s, pictorial representation of Lumumba came to unite holy or religious history with political history through the figure of Lumumba as Christ. This metaphor gave rise to the popular memory of Lumumba as a martyr who underwent his ordeal willingly. The images narrate an "end of history" that is transformed into a day of judgment. In this narrative, Christianity and populism—a populism inspired by leftist ideologies of the 1960s, which at the time fueled such movements as pan-Africanism, Third-Worldism, and antiimperialism—are closely intertwined. Local urban memory thus appropriates bits of universalist discourse. In this representation Lumumba immolates himself on the altar of his own words, the words of his June 30, 1960 speech, and on the great hopes that the speech inspired, hopes that memory has guarded, reproduced, and re-created in the image of people's present sensibilities—namely, the promise of dignity and sovereignty. In Katangese popular painting, Lumumba is presented as the incarnation of these two promises, which are also actions: breaking the chains of slavery and becoming human beings whose right to justice is *recognized,* and with it their equality with all other such beings. Over the past four decades these two promises have continued to be of utmost relevance for the Congolese.

For the outside viewer, Lumumba as Christ, as a man who underwent Christ's passion, constitutes the key to the narrative. It seems to me that the painting by Tshibumba that portrays a Christ with Lumumba's facial (fig.67) features is meant above all to guide such outside viewers. It gives the person who does not share this memory a key with

Fig. 59.
Photographic print of Lumumba distributed by Mouvement National Congolais-Lumumba in 1960.

which to penetrate the secret common to the members of the group. In this culture, a social actor moderately familiar with Congolese collective memory would never utter anything so obvious as "Lumumba is Christ," for the statement would offend people's aesthetic sensibility and call into doubt the speaker's authenticity. In 1998, Burozi, the Likasi painter from whom Tshibumba learned his craft, painted all the subjects he had written down in his notebook, including the historical cycle encompassing the death of Lumumba. Burozi's painting of Lumumba's death (fig. 32) is much less explicit than Tshibumba's. It is dominated by the figure of the soldier on the right, resting after his hard labor, and on the left by the shovels that have just been used to dig the grave. The bodies are sketched in at the center, of course, but even though their spatial arrangement is a clear allusion to Christ and his two companions, one has to know *already* that the Christ figure here is actually Lumumba. As Burozi himself explained, he only worked for a local clientele. (He receives few commissions now and has become a full-time preacher.)

The narrative metaphor is developed and deployed in communication between painters and their clientele. As mentioned, the point of departure for this art is a few images that function as icons: Lumumba breaking chains (the chains of slavery); Lumumba, the reincarnation of Christ, stepping out of an airplane to undergo his martyrdom; Lumumba, whose very voice makes injustice tremble; and Lumumba, master of the earth. This last icon suggests that in the local conception of the Trinity there is a kind of equivalence between God's three persons: God can take on the appearance of any one of them, and even that of an ordinary being on whom His grace has descended. In the last painting, for instance, we see Lumumba's human flesh receiving the divine presence. He is the master of the world, which he holds in his hands, and he himself has chosen to be martyred to redeem humanity.

Attributing political ancestors to Lumumba from before independence (or even ancestors who lived before the whites arrived) makes it possible to free the metaphor from the images and symbols imposed on it by the colonial and postcolonial states. Not only are the Promethean and Congolese sides of Lumumba emphasized, but autonomous Congolese historicity is restored. Because the culture that functions this way is a Christian one, saintly history, impelled by political history, can reach back to a time before Lumumba. The timeline leading from Western missionary Christianity to local, syncretic Christianity can thus be reversed, and Lumumba's action can be projected back into the time before colonial occupation. This is the ethical principle at work, which here infuses the historical Lumumba, providing him with a springboard into the political future.

FIG. 60.
Lumumba arriving in Elisabethville (Torment).
By Mutanda wa Mutanda.
Oil on fabric, 15 x 23¼ in.

With the exception of the paintings in which Lumumba's status as a respectable man is indicated by his personal elegance, a single formal arrangement dominates most paintings of him. The pictorial space is organized on the model of the Catholic altar, an aesthetic of the Trinity ordered by symmetry and repetition. In both Lumumba's "passion" as painted by Tshibumba and the depiction of his arrival at Elisabethville (Lubumbashi) as painted by several different artists, the image is symmetrical in relation to the median axis. The most frequently painted moment is Lumumba's arrival at his final destination: he is shown descending from the plane that has brought him to Elisabethville to meet his destiny,

FIG. 61.
Calvaire d'Afrique. [Torment of Africa, also called "National Hero and Prophet of Our Liberation"]. By Tshibumba. Oil on fabric, 18¹/₂ x 35 in. Verbeek Collection.

arriving at the final "Station of the Cross," soon to undergo martyrdom. It is a canonical image in Katangese popular painting; I have seen more than a hundred examples of this modern version of the Stations of the Cross—modern because it took place for the most part during the flight over the Congo, the country be liberated from colonial chains. It culminates, as we know, in torture and death.

The scene of prisoner Lumumba's arrival at Elisabethville is implicitly inscribed in modern times by the airplane, and by the men in suits and hats in the background (figs. 60, 61). Lumumba himself wears a simple undergarment, a singlet, which signifies both that he is Christ carrying the cross and that he is an equal of ordinary Congolese. Lumumba belongs to the people. Meanwhile his striped pants, which evoke the coat-and-tails evening dress of which they are a part, denote his elegance. With the exception of a helmet and military stripes, Lumumba is here painted as Clément described him in 1952 on his way to visit a local Belgian administrator: an *évolué,* an agent of the state, an elegant man. Even the Belgian press acknowledged that Lumumba was "elegantly dressed" *(La Libre Belgique,* November 11, 1959; quoted in Masuy 1997:202).

Lumumba's arms are tied behind his back with a rope, a foreshadowing of his martyrdom. The soldiers, who number between two and four and frame him to the right and left, are meant more as his companions; they are figures not of executioners but of the two thieves crucified with Christ. The body of the martyr divides the pictorial space of the lower part of the painting (its foreground) into two equal parts, so that it is Lumumba himself who constitutes the dominant axis. He looks directly at the viewer. Framed by black soldiers, he shares with them the space of the world of the ordinary Congolese—the space of the tortured prisoner in the "Belgian Colony" icon. This icon, the most widespread denunciation of state injustice, dominates popular painting.

The top of the painting contains a different political universe. In the upper right, a small group of actors represent a single "personage," that of the Katangese secession. They stand for the "white" in the "Belgian Colony" icon. In the upper left we see an airplane. The modernity that Lumumba promised the Congolese they would master, but that also contributed to his downfall, is outside the space of the ordinary Congolese man; it crushes him. Only the politicians may come close to or share this space.

FIG. 62.
Allegory of independant Congo, the woman
symbolizes the future and the rooster, the
Movement National Congolais-Lumumba.
By Ange Kumm. Oil on fabric, 20½ x 26½ in.

While the tragedy is played out in the foreground, the middle ground seems neutral.
The airplane is associated with the state by means of the inscription it bears: "Sabena,"
"Air Congo," even "République Congolaise." As for the group of men (usually three)
who occupy that space, their clothes and accessories, such as attaché cases, indicate
that they are politicians. They are there like Pontius Pilate after he delivered Christ to
the Jews, "legalizing" the political murder, although not participating in it directly. This
too is a reference to the "Belgian Colony." And just as the plane points to the responsibility of those who betrayed Lumumba (including Mobutu, though he is not named), so
the presence of the group of politicians refers to the responsibility of the Katangese,
the same who in 1960–61 excluded the Kasaians and the Luba Katanga from that local
space. It is interesting to see how close this element of the icon is to Césaire's stage
directions for *Une Saison au Congo* (Césaire 1993:113). In the final scene of the play,
when the lights come back on, we a see "a group of people who have literally been
turned into statues": *les banquiers* (the bankers), Kala (Joseph Kasa-Vubu), Tzumbi
(Tshombe), Mokutu (Mobutu) and, off to the side, Dag Hammarskjöld.

Tshibumba and the other popular painters did not invent the representation of
Lumumba as Christ, but translated it into visual language and integrated it into an aesthetic that transforms the event into tragedy. International literature, especially that of
black Francophone writers, also portrays Lumumba as Christ, speaking of his martyrdom
and his passion, his crucifixion and resurrection, and the apocalypse that would follow
his death (Hoyet 1993:53).

FIG. 63.
Gendarmes Katangais. [Katangese soldiers
(forcing MNC-L supporter to eat the party
bulletin)]. By Burozi. Oil on fabric, 15¼ x 19¼

Fig. 64.
*Patrice Emery Lumumba, son esprit incarné dans
Mze Liberateur. Mzee Laurent Désiré Kabila, Le
libérateur de la R.D.C.* [Patrice Emery Lumumba,
his spirit is incarnated in Mze Liberator.
Mzee Laurent Desire Kabila, the liberator
of the Democratic Republic of Congo.].
By A.B.C. Banza, 1998. Oil on fabric, 33 x 24 in.

Fig 65.
Patrice Emery Lumumba. By Tshibumba.
Oil on fabric, 26¼ x 19¼ in.

Political Change and New Representations of Lumumba

Several recent paintings reinterpret the figure of the hero according to the sensibility of the last few years. Burozi, probably the oldest living popular painter in Katanga, has painted Lumumba as part of a Congolese national trinity, next to the first Congolese Christian prophet, Simon Kimbangu, and the first president of the Congo, Kasa-Vubu. The arrangement of the three heads recalls popular religious paintings of God the Father creating the world, but it was also inspired by the effigy of Mobutu descending from the clouds that used to appear as a fixed image on Zairian television in the 1980s at the beginning of every televised newscast. Urban memory and certain autonomous local churches have sanctified Lumumba, presenting Kimbangu as a Congolese Saint John the Baptist who preceded and announced Lumumba-Christ's coming. And in *Une Saison au Congo,* Césaire has his *sanza* player say to Lumumba,

> You are our inspired guide, our messiah!
> Grace be to God, my children—
> Simon Kimbangu is among us once again!

FIG. 66.
Patrice Emery Lumumba, Mzee Kabila, Moïse Tshombe, Kasa-Vubu. By A.B.C. Banza., 1998. Oil on fabric, 27 x 42½ in.

A painting done in Kinshasa in 1996 puts together a rooster and a female bust—according to the artist, woman represents the future of the country (fig. 62). It is probable that the rooster (fig. 63), an animal regularly used for divination purposes, is a reference to the *sanza* player who in Césaire's play is described as a divining rooster. Toward the end of the play, the sanza player drops dead, like a sacrificial cock, before Mokutu (Mobutu), to denounce his role in Lumumba's death.

These connections between black African literature and popular Congolese imagination may seem arbitrary, but it must not be forgotten that several Congolese painters are what could be called intellectuals of the people, who collect and read all that may help them to paint. Used books and old illustrated magazines are sold very cheaply on city sidewalks in Congo, and educated people read all they can get their hands on in the hope of increasing their knowledge. Painters may be inspired by a bit of text they've read, or by the memory of a conversation they have had with someone who's read it.

Lumumba as Christ has dominated the ethical conception of politics, but recently the way seems to have been paved for a more abstract, less narrative script (fig. 65). When a script is more detached from narrative, it can perhaps better facilitate a shared national political image that opens onto a sort of reconciliation between all the fathers of independence—all of whom, it should be noted, are claimed to be both ancestors and companions of Kabila. A painting done at Lubumbashi in the fall of 1998, just before the new war afforded Kabila an undreamed-of national legitimacy, shows four leaders on two axes (fig. 66): the vertical Katangese axis of Tshombe and Kabila, and the horizontal Congolese axis of Lumumba and Kasa-Vubu. Another painting places Lumumba in a cloud (fig. 64), the position that Zairian television reserved for Mobutu-the-supreme-guide, while Kabila, Lumumba's descendant, emerges from around the outline of the country—the place that in the past was reserved for Lumumba. Should we conclude from this that at least in the urban memory of Lubumbashi, Lumumba is no longer of this world; that his body has finally been buried and mourning for him ended, permitting the hero to take his place as an ancestor and to yield his place on earth to Kabila, a unitarist Katangese? It would be a mistake to interpret these few paintings, for which there are no local buyers at present, as a reflection of some new understanding, for as I write, new memory is groping in the midst of events whose meaning is uncertain. Meanwhile Congolese men and women focus all their efforts on biological survival.

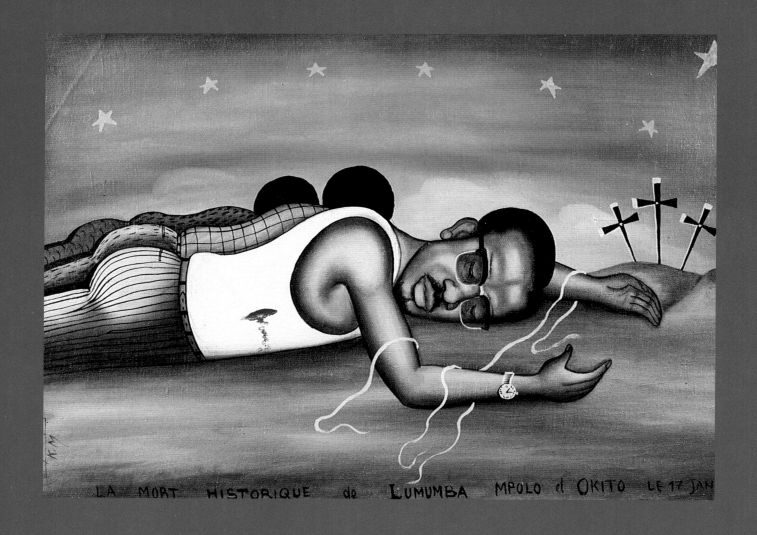

LA MORT HISTORIQUE de LUMUMBA MPOLO et OKITO LE 17 JAN

Anticipation and Longing: Congolese Culture Heroes Past, Present, and Future

by Mary Nooter Roberts and Allen F. Roberts

The measure of a hero is "the continual possibilization of possibles."
—Jean-Paul Sartre, *Being and Nothingness (1956)*

Narrative paintings like those of Tshibumba Kanda-Matulu possess ukumbusho—"the ability to cause to remember" in Swahili.[1] In the mid-1970s, this is how urbanites in southern Congo [Zaire] described the active nature of such images, as the pictures "occasioned talk and prompted stories" from the communally shared memories of "past experiences and present predicaments" (Fabian 1998:64; idem, 1996:195).[2] Yet, despite the fact that painting on "canvas" (usually made from flour sacks) is a recent expressive form in this part of Africa, such a dynamic capacity did not emerge in colonial or postcolonial times. Rather, it is derived from earlier senses of the efficacy of "art" and systems of mnemonic experience held by Luba and related peoples.

At first glance, the colorful, emotive scenes in Tshibumba's urban paintings seem to have little in common with the seemingly stoic royal sculptures from rural lands where Luba created an important precolonial state (figs. 68, 69). Yet, familiarity with the critical points of convergence and continuity between these traditions allows a deeper understanding of Congolese historical consciousness, and the uses of art in memory processes past and present.

Precolonial ideologies and political structures of Luba, Tabwa, Lunda, Chokwe, and related southern Congolese groups were buttressed by a rich body of oral literature and associated objects and performances that served as arts of memory. Luba peoples of southern Congo possess a most complex and sophisticated mnemonic system (Roberts and Roberts 1996). In the eighteenth century, Luba kings founded an institution dedicated to collective memory and historical knowledge through objects and actions. These included *lukasa* wooden memory boards for the recall of complex historical facts and royal precepts; accouterments, body arts, and staffs of office whose iconography could be used to recount chiefly narratives (fig. 70, 71); dances that enacted episodes from the Luba epic; and tone poems, songs, and other music-making, esoteric allusions to ancient spirits and arcane maxims. Luba political culture, imagery, and performances were and still are enlivened by devices such as these that date back several centuries (see Childs and Maret 1996). They assist recitations of king lists, genealogies, and the great Luba epic, and support assertions of primacy and political legitimacy by competing factions, clans, and individual leaders. Contestation was rife during the nineteenth century due to internal rivalries and pressures from the east African ivory and slave trade that encroached upon Luba frontiers; and sadly, some of these same patterns of conflict re-emerged in the 1970s and have increased through the 1990s.[3]

FIG. 67.
La mort historique de Lumumba, Mpolo et Okoto le 17 Janv. 1961 [Historic Death of Lumumba, Mpolo and Okito, on 17 January 1961]. By Tshibumba, K.M. Oil on fabric, 14½ x 22 in.

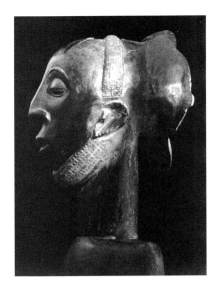

In contrast to these earlier expressive forms, popular painting in southern Congo was developed in the mid- twentieth century for an urban petite bourgeoisie.[4] The medium shifted from sculpture and performance to painting because of the influences of beaux-arts training and the readily available imagery of mass-produced religious tracts, newspapers, comic books, and advertisements (see Fabian 1996:300-306, and Jewsiewicki 1996). The emphasis also shifted from regional roots to an emerging nationalist consciousness among a population with memories of colonial brutalities and the secessionist violence of the 1960s (Jewsiewicki 1991:130). In the 1970s, genre paintings were purchased and displayed by young urbanites seeking relief from the cruel absurdities of President Mobutu's administration, and the inequities and iniquities of capitalist success or failure.[5]

Tshibumba's painted portrayal of political figures, such as Patrice Lumumba, as "culture heroes" has deep antecedents in the artist's own Luba heritage. Culture heroes for Luba and many other African peoples have often been presented in Western literature as bearers of innovative ideas, technologies, and political systems.[6] Yet, the individuals identified by outside observers as "culture heroes" in both precolonial and postcolonial Congolese contexts are not simply personae as much as they are processes, performances, and "events" personified by and for people in the present. A comparison of contemporary painting and precolonial sculpture and performance demonstrates that the memory of culture heroes is not a one-way projection into the past, but an enactment in the present of what *will have been*. Acting in the "future perfect," culture heroes embody change by stimulating anticipation and longing. Their nomadic ways further transcend the bounded geographies of space, time, and gender.

Arguments to be presented here have been influenced by the study of culture heroes in other parts of Africa and elsewhere, and useful comparison can be drawn to the way that saints function in religions around the world to structure experience and lend moral sense to everyday lives (Wyschograd 1990).[7]

Saints exact devotion from their followers through the force of hagiographic texts. Hagiography is the biography of a saintly life, but rather than mere description, hagiography is a practice that causes the reader to become swept up by the narrative in such a way that his/her life becomes an extension of the saint's (Wyschograd 1990). At issue is what Johannes Fabian calls a "way with time" driven more by consequence than sequence, so that instead of a Western-style historiography, there results a "historiology: the shared memories of colonial and postcolonial history objectified in written texts, oral accounts, and visual images" (Fabian 1998:88, 94, 96, elaborating on a term proposed by Jan Vansina). As Edith Wyschograd (1990:xxiii) asserts, saints' lives do not merely exist; they are constructed and reconstructed in endless refabulation, in much the same way that the Luba epic is enacted rather than simply reenacted through each successive investiture ceremony, every initiation rite, and the night of the new moon each month of every year when the culture heroes come to life through trance and other forms of embodied memory. In this way, hagiography is a narrative form that possesses its own vitality, ensuring that the life of the hero or saint is forever perpetuated in the changing present, and that the present is continuously grafted onto the pure potentiality of a remembered past.

Memory and History in Contest

As an emerging literature demonstrates, memory is neither universal nor monolithic.[8] Instead, memory is socially and temporally constructed to reflect the values and ideologies of particular periods and places. Memory must be perceived from the various points of view generated within different cultures. For example, there are striking similarities between *ukumbusho* in Congolese urban artistic contexts, early Luba concepts and practices of memory, and postmodern meditations on memory and history. In all three cases, memory is perceived as an active, performative process serving to stimulate the creation of histories (Roberts and Roberts 1996; Fabian 1996, 1998). This perception differs from earlier Western notions of memory as a representation of Truth, in a positivist sense of the word, or as a passive databank of the mind from which information can be retrieved. Memory is now understood to be creative and negotiable, and the histories derived from it are contingent upon changing social and economic circumstances. As Valentin Mudimbe has written, "history is a legend, an invention of the present" (1988:195)—and memory is always *now*.

Whereas memory may be an amorphous watercolor wash of collective remembrances, history is always a deliberately linear selection of events that will serve to legitimate a political position, status, or platform. Pierre Nora (1989) discusses the tension between history and memory, for history ceaselessly attempts to suppress memory because it holds the potential to subvert any particular history. Zairian popular paintings, with their personal and collective visions of colonial experience, articulate the tensions and conflicts between memory and history, and between history as told, versus history as written. When Tshibumba Kanda-Matulu produced more than one hundred paintings in his "History of Zaire" series, his artistic departures from "facts" were intended to "make us think"; they were, as Fabian puts it, "fictions with a message" (1996:xiii). In this sense, memory is an art of rhetoric, debate, and strategy, rather than an "abstract presentation of truth" (Fabian 1983:112).

Tshibumba's concept of history was "to work something out in his mind." This was no mere handing down of memories passively received, then, but rather a purposeful, political, and intellectual activity of "selecting events, arranging their sequence, and representing them in painting" (Fabian 1996:311). The notion of "working it out" is reminiscent of a Luba assertion that history is like a "stringing together of beads" for a necklace (from the verb *kulanga)* to tell a particular story (Roberts and Roberts 1996:29). Indeed, beaded necklaces are one of the primary insignia of Luba office, and chiefs can "read" and recite lengthy genealogies and other histories through the positioning of beads on their regalia (Nkindi and De Plaen 1996). Recollection, as practiced by Luba, is neither an account nor a pedigree, but a meaningful configuration of selected events around "loci of memory" or lieux de mémoire (Jewsiewicki and Mudimbe 1993:10; Nora 1984; Roberts and Roberts 1996:38). A *lieu de mémoire* is a landmark around which past events structure present memory. As actual and imagined places, *lieux de mémoire* are topoi—that

is, "both places and topics, where memories converge" (Blok 1991:125). Luba beads are signifiers for just such *lieux de mémoire*: people and events in the past that can be reorganized, reconfigured, and reinterpreted to update histories for identity making and problem-solving *in the present* (Roberts and Roberts 1996:Introduction).[9]

Culture Heroes as *Lieux de Mémoire*

One of the key characteristics of *lieux de mémoire* is their intimate link to both physical geography and the human body. Ever since classical times, historians have acknowledged the importance of place for the recall of historical events. Memory arts *(ars memoria)* were based upon memory places *(loci memoriae)* that could be "seen" and "visited" in the mind. To remember their speeches, ancient orators imagined buildings and assigned topics and subtopics to the "rooms" through which they would mentally "walk" as they delivered their talks (Yates 1966). In this sense, memory has topographic fixity, but temporal evanescence. Past events can be enacted at any time, as long as they are lodged or "emplaced" in a locus of sustainable embodiment, such as a structure, a body, or a work of art.[10]

Bogumil Jewsiewicki applies the model of *lieux de mémoire* to the culture heroes of popular painting (this volume). The firebrand Patrice Lumumba is a locus around whom southern Congolese urban memory reconfigures itself in genre paintings of a specifically political nature. By the mid-1970s, Lumumba emerges as a *lieu de mémoire* for a nationalist consciousness because of the well-known contention between him and Mobutu that led to Lumumba's martyrdom, and because he incarnates the struggle for dignity, modernity, and political and ontological independence. Yet, attitudes toward Lumumba vary among ethnic groups and factions at different times according to political and ideological positions regarding particular issues, such as the secession of Katanga versus national unity. A *lieu de mémoire*, then, can be divided—a symbol of opposed, even contested loyalties, depending upon the relationships, associations, and connections between it and competing *lieu de mémoire*.

Events further demonstrate how *lieux de mémoire* engender memory in the present. The representation of a specific moment, such as the scene depicted in Tshibumba's "The Historic Death of Lumumba" (fig. 69, p.92), blends past and present "to invoke the force of collective memory in the present" (Jules-Rosette 1992:57). Bennetta Jules-Rosette describes the painting's visual allegory as a plea to Congolese to assess their contemporary situation. Violence has visibly occurred, yet it is conflated with the redemptive messages of Christianity (Jewsiewicki 1996). Through allusion to the Resurrection, Tshibumba tacitly tells his viewers that a better future can be anticipated. Likewise, in the well-known painting "Colonie belge," that depicts the horrors of colonial abuse against the background of an idyllic village setting (fig. 8, p.18), and in other paintings casting specific historical moments of struggle and liberation amidst scenes of contemporary Lubumbashi, Tshibumba deliberately blurs temporal sequences. He draws upon "signs of the times" to transcend history in order to empower people to act. As Jules-Rosette (1992:58) explains:

> popular painting plays upon the specificity of collective memory and action by referencing particular historical occurrences and myths. At the same time, it transcends these concrete referents through its use of visual signs to create a reality effect . . . that invokes a timeless sense of the social imaginary in which past, present, and future blend in an ongoing unity. The "Colonie belge" genre has no specific meaning as a mere monument to history. Rather, "Colonie belge" is creative expression instead of commemorative art; it is an active representation of the present and a warning of things to come.[11]

In this sense, a culture hero's life is "doubly coded" with respect to time. It exists in both the past and future tenses simultaneously, or more precisely in a combination of the two, producing the future anterior tense of "what will have been." Like culture heroes, Wyschograd observes that saints exist two times at once—the time of work and achievement that defines their mission, and a time of "pure flux or passage" in which a saint loses him/herself to the Other. A saint's or hero's life is an irrecoverable or lapsed time, "a flux that passes away and that constitutes the temporal framework of the saint's relation with the Other" (1990:xxiii).[12]

Precolonial Culture Heroes

Luba precolonial political history situates itself around numerous *lieux de mémoire* that shape attitudes about power, identity, and spirituality in the present.[13] In ways analogous to Lumumba's appropriation by different ethnicities, constituencies, and generations, the heroes of the precolonial epic serve the interests of competing factions in the ongoing revision and performance of history.

The Luba epic, which has been transcribed many times and is now included in secondary school history books in the Congo, recounts how a culture hero named Mbidi Kiluwe came from the east bringing kingship, new technologies, and the etiquette of courtly bearing to Luba people.[14] Until that time, Luba were oppressed by a ruthless despot named Nkongolo Mwamba, whose skin was "red" like the hot blood of violence. If Nkongolo is lord of every excess, from incest to parricide and tyranny; Mbidi is the cool, "black" hero who stands for all that is measured, just and good, civilized, sophisticated, and progressive. In one version, Nkongolo's sister weds Mbidi and bears him a son named Kalala Ilunga. Kalala grows to become a clever and valiant warrior who overthrows his cruel uncle to become the first Luba king of historical times. Yet in his descent, Kalala embodies the opposing forces of Nkongolo's "red" abandon and Mbidi's "black" wisdom, and thus he incarnates the paradoxes, tensions, and struggles inherent to politics and social change (A. Roberts 1991). The fusion of these qualities in the person of the king is a statement about the ambivalence of power, which is as potentially productive and beneficent as it can be selfish and destructive (Heusch 1982a; Mudimbe 1991, 1996; A. Roberts 1991).

Luba peoples remember the details of this heroic epic through several mnemonic devices, the most important of which is a lukasa memory board. A lukasa is a wooden board inscribed with carved ideograms or studded with colorful glass beads, shells, and metal pins in configurations that provide cues for "men of memory" as they recite the epic during investiture of kings and chiefs, initiation of officeholders, and other important court rituals (fig. 72). While a lukasa is used to recount the history of a kingdom, that history can nevertheless be told from a variety of vantage points, in ways similar to how Tshibumba's popular paintings of Lumumba can be interpreted according to the political motives of the beholder. Each chiefdom of the Luba polity possessed its own lukasa and its own branch of the Mbudye royal historical society. Men of memory from any region could narrate events through the eyes and following the interests of their own leaders, factions, and clans. Still today, in rural areas of the Luba heartland, chiefs and their dignitaries sometimes use lukasas as they spend hours debating different interpretations of the epic, denouncing the way that history has been told by those asserting rival claims to some valued prerogative and offering instead their own "authentic" explanations (Nooter 1991: Ch.3).

Fig. 72.
Two members of the Mbudye historical association are shown here with a staff and a lukasa memory board. A lukasa is a device to assist court historians with the recall of the Luba epic and the kinglists that validate descendance from the culture heroes, Mbidi Kiluwe and Kalala Ilunga. Photo: Mary Nooter Roberts, Shaba Region, Democratic Republic of Congo, 1989.

The epic was appropriated by or shared with peoples far from the Luba heartland. Not only do Luba-related groups claim the same heroes as their own, but neighboring or distant peoples such as Tabwa, Bemba, Lunda, and Chokwe have constructed their political systems on extensions and inversions of the Luba epic. Lunda and Chokwe oral histories, for example, attribute the origins of royalty to the son of a Lunda queen named Lueji and a Luba hunter called Chibinda Ilunga, who by many accounts was Kalala Ilunga's son (Turner 1955).[15] Lueji is the structural equivalent of Nkongolo Mwamba (Heusch 1982a:151, 155), and she and Chibinda Ilunga "personify the two antagonistic principles in the dualistic ideology of sovereignty . . . one principle emphasizing autochthony and ancestry . . . while an opposing principle emphasizes the innovating order" (Palmeirim 1998:21). As Mbidi Kiluwe and Kalala Ilunga had for Luba, Chibinda introduces Lunda and Chokwe to noble forms of chieftaincy, and it is from Chibinda that Lunda and Chokwe kings and chiefs claim descent.

Of odd significance is that in all these cases, the hero hails from "a world of elsewhere" (Heusch 1991:109). Wyschograd (1990) similarly notes that a signal characteristic of saints is their absence of fixed dwelling. A saint is often a nomad without known origin and without particular destination. Luba, Lunda, and Chokwe culture heroes always come from "somewhere to the east," and often from "the other side of the river" or beyond other boundaries (Roberts 1980, 1991; Heusch 1982a, 1991). Mbidi Kiluwe and Chibinda Ilunga are travelers, and their historical roles are based on fugitive encounters during which they introduce startlingly innovative social orders, only to disappear enigmatically, once again (Roberts 1993). The divesting of home is part of what makes these heroes and saints sentient beings of such striking "corporeal vulnerability" (Wyschograd 1990:83).

FIG. 73.
Figure of Chibinda Ilunga (or a chief embodying him). Chokwe people, Angola. 19th century. Wood. H. 14 in. The Stanley Collection of The University of Iowa Museum of Art, collected in Angola around 1895. In some precolonial cultures of central Africa, culture heroes take literal form as sculpted human figures. Here Chibinda Ilunga, the paragon of Chokwe kingship and son of the Luba culture hero Kalala Ilunga, is shown with a dramatic royal headdress and enlarged hands that hold male and female ancestors.

Imaging Culture Heroes

While precolonial Congolese political developments in this region are based upon the same or closely related origin stories and culture heroes, there is significant variation in the ways that the heroes are imaged in art and performance. Chokwe peoples, whose homelands in southwestern Congo, northwestern Zambia, and eastern Angola, are far from the Luba heartland, produce sculptures that depict Chibinda Ilunga as the Luba hunter-hero-culture-bearer who introduced kingship (Bastin 1978; Heusch 1988; Jordán 1998:29 and Plates 1, 3, 5). The hero is shown as a physically powerful male figure wearing a spectacular headdress, and holding in each hand the emblems of the hunt, or smaller figures. These figures depict a chief and his wife as the male and female aspects of rulership, and/or the ancestral spirits that uphold the chiefdom as a whole (Jordán 1998:32) (fig. 73). Such important objects are both aesthetically and conceptually rich for they offer an explicit image of the hero and the principles for which he stands. They presuppose knowledge of the epics, and such narrative "annotates the physical portrait of the saint [or hero] with the 'inner' portrait of his or her virtues" (Belting 1994:257). What is more, the figures possess an exacting presence, for through "godly inherence" (Freedberg 1989:35), Chibinda is *there* where his figure is emplaced, demanding propriety of action according to established norms (M. Jordán pers. comm. 1997; Roberts and Roberts 1997:17).

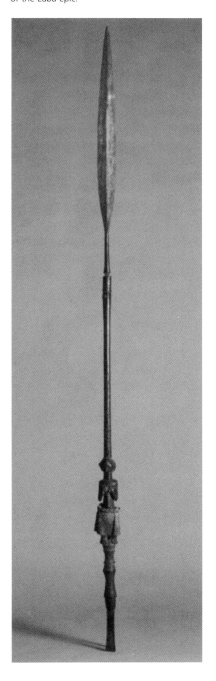

FIG. 74.
Ceremonial Spear, Luba peoples, Democratic Republic of Congo. 19th century. Wood, iron, cloth. H. 61 in. The Stanley Collection of The University of Iowa Museum of Art. While Luba peoples do not depict their culture heroes in literal terms, they do commemorate them sculpturally through replicas of the insignia that they possessed. Spears recall the culture hero's introduction of advanced metalworking technologies to Luba and critical incidents of the Luba epic.

Although Chokwe peoples derive their royal practices from Lunda, they express royalty through a flourishing sculptural tradition, whereas Lunda do not prioritize sculpture over other arts. Lunda history and expressive culture focus on oral traditions and related performances that explain the currency of the exploits of culture bearers, and on beaded accouterments and regalia that are not primarily sculptural but that are no less sacred than objects like Chokwe figures of Chibinda Ilunga.[16] The most potent visual symbols of Lunda rulership that provide the most direct connection to culture heroes are a beaded crown and a sacred bracelet called *rukan (lukano)* made of human sinew, that Lueji gave to Chibinda Ilunga when they fell in love. The bracelet is worn only by Lunda kings (Palmeirim 1998:21-27), although on at least one occasion, Chokwe are said to have stolen the bracelet and therefore the source of royal authenticity. Other articles of dress and status worn by paramounts and their dignitaries convey the symbolic divisions and tensions between the new social order and the previous political system, or refer to specific historical incidents legitimizing current prerogatives. In other words, the deeds and attributes of Lunda culture heroes are not depicted as free-standing sculptures as in the Chokwe case, but as symbolic referents in the form of clothing or insignia that serve as reminders of royal origins as narrated in oral accounts (ibid:24-27).

Luba do produce an abundance of sculpture related to kingship, but almost always in the form of elaborated weapons of the hunt, tools of smelting and blacksmithing, or others that serve as royal implements and insignia. Spears and staffs, axes and knives, headrests and thrones are the objects that the Luba culture heroes possessed and passed down to Luba kings (fig. 74). Present-day Luba rulers and dignitaries claim that these beautifully elaborated objects are replicas of the original insignia belonging to Mbidi Kiluwe and Kalala Ilunga. It is our contention that Luba political actors do not possess, commission, or patronize images that depict the culture heroes as do Chokwe peoples, because Luba rulers legitimize themselves through their capacity to incarnate and personify the culture heroes *directly,* through rituals and trance states in contexts of investiture, divination, and problem-solving. Their insignia serve to complete the dramatic incarnation of the heroes by actual Luba kings, chiefs, diviners, and dignitaries in the present (figs. 76, 77).

To understand how and why a culture chooses a particular manner of representing its heroes at a particular time requires an understanding of how people conceive of their heroes. Luba assert that Mbidi Kiluwe did exist and that the epic is true history, while outside observers may consider him metaphorical or legendary. Colonial administrator Edmund Verhulpen (1936) attributed the historicity of bounded "empires" to both Nkongolo Mwamba and Kalala Ilunga, thus condensing whole epochs into the person of either ruler. Africanist historian Jan Vansina (1966) considers the culture heroes to have been historical figures, thus challenging a prevailing Western assumption that African accounts of origin are mythical. Structuralist anthropologist Luc de Heusch (1982a, 1982b) sees in the epic a complex cosmological system shared among Bantu-speaking peoples of central and southern Africa, based upon principles of opposition and mediation. Philosopher/social critic Valentin Mudimbe blurs such symmetry by perceiving the ambiguity inherent in the dual nature of power and personhood embodied by the culture heroes: "The body contains two conflictual inheritances; and from generation to generation, it has been rearticulated and recomposed, realizing and assuming itself in the opposing expectations of each social formation" (Mudimbe 1996:246). More critical than the historical veracity of the culture heroes is their ability to engender history in the present and create "what will have been" in the here and now (Roberts and Roberts 1996).

Fig. 75.
Janus Figure. Kusu peoples, Democratic Republic of Congo. 19th century. Wood, horn, metal tacks and nails, medicinal ingredients. H. 13½ in. The Stanley Collection of The University of Iowa Museum of Art. That culture heroes bridge past and present, and embody a future perfect sense is reflected by Janus figures that look in two directions at once. Medicine activates the threshold between revered past and perfected future, to instigate choice and change.

Fig. 76.
A chief and his son stand in state holding the emblems of their office, which they claim derive directly from the first Luba king, Kalala Ilunga. A spear and a staff were among the insignia that Kalala Ilunga's father—the preeminent culture hero, Mbidi Kiluwe—left to his son and subsequent generations. Photo: Mary Nooter Roberts, Shaba Region, Democratic Republic of Congo, 1989.

An Aesthetics of Anticipation

The name of the Luba culture hero reveals an ontology of the "future perfect." "Mbidi" means "melanistic serval" in the Luba language, with reference to a feline so elusive that it can be present without being seen. In the 1970s, people sometimes included pieces of *mbidi* pelt in invisibility magic to escape the notice of Mobutu's soldiers or the brigands of his political party (A. Roberts 1986a). The black cat makes further apt reference to the "black" secrecy of the culture hero, who is the master of all that is arcane, artfully indirect, and beyond the obvious (idem 1993:71-73). Mbidi is everything that *might* be known and is by the initiated, and he embodies the unlimited potentialities of memory itself (idem 1996:241).

Mbidi's second name, "Kiluwe," refers to a paradigm of dichotomous beings found throughout central Africa.[17] These may be presented in narratives concerning heroes whose one half is human while the other is made of beeswax or absent altogether (idem 1993:73-74). Sometimes (though not by Luba), such heroes and related spirits are depicted in sculpture as half-beings (e.g. a Chokwe figure illustrated in Jordán 1998: Plate 115). The one half longs for completion by re/gaining its other. The tension produced by yearning can be made instrumental in magic. We suspect that a Pare half-figure (fig. 81) now in the Stanley Collection of the University of Iowa (Roy 1992:251) may have been a material manifestation of someone's intention to seek resolution to a problem.

In his dichotomous anatomy, Mbidi Kiluwe embodies both paradox and dialectic. Presence implies absence, form formlessness, asymmetry symmetry, visibility that which is hidden. Divided beings capture the ever-so-abstract threshold of a fleeting present, always on the verge: Of what? The threshold's fine line *between* demands choice, decision, and creativity (A. Roberts 1992). "Mediators are fundamental," Gilles Deleuze tells us. "Creation is all about mediators. Without them, nothing happens" (1992:285). We are reminded of the nineteenth-century Hindu saint Paramahansa Ramakrishna's once being asked, "Where do I find God?" and of his haunting reply, "Look between two thoughts" (Shearer 1993:16).

African arts are often marked and motivated by thresholds.[18] In the "in-between" of the threshold, people contemplate difference and transformation as they speak in riddles and conundra, celebrate ambiguities through visual and performed arts, narrate perplexing dilemma tales, and dramatize transition through ritual. Two-faced Janus masks and figures make tangible and accessible the ineffable concept of the threshold (fig. 75).

Janus was the ancient Roman god of thresholds and passages (Schilling 1960), and the name "Janus" is derived from an Indo-European root meaning "to pass by, on, or through" (ibid.:91). Cicero suggested that as "the deification of movement," Janus is "engaged with his double face in an eternal becoming" (Grimal 1945:21). Janus thereby engages time, and especially the transition from one month to the next, for he is identified with the interlunium—the two or three nights of darkness between a last sighting of the passing month's moon and a first glimmer of the new moon rising.[19] Like Janus, Mbidi Kiluwe is a lunar hero whose alternation of enlightened and obscure sides launches the cycles of civilization. After all, for Luba "the moon is as ambiguous as life itself. . . . The unknown is at the heart of the ordinary. To be and become, to live and to die, are but two faces of the same reality" (Theuws 1968:11).

Bifrontal figures and masks are quite common in central Africa (A. Roberts 1986b), and among their references is the same sort of temporal sense conveyed by the Roman god (fig. 79). The faces of Janus figures and masks look backward and forward, from revered past to perfected future, as Manuel Jordán (1993) was explicitly told by the Chokwe ritual expert who had constructed a Janus mask depicting the primordial Chokwe queen Lweji. Often, magic is placed at the threshold between Janus faces, to activate the threshold's creative power of hypothesis, choice, and change (A. Roberts 1986b). The person addressing a Janus spirit or performing a Janus masquerade enacts prolepsis—"the device of anticipation . . . [that] produces a synopsis of two feelings and two time planes" (Belting 1994:285), and so "represents something in the future as if it already existed or had occurred" (Flexner 1987:1547). In other words, one recalls ancient models of propriety and courage introduced by culture heroes like Mbidi Kiluwe, as one acts now to enjoy a future that "will have been" as fulfilling as the collective memories of those halcyon times. Longing for a better life is matched by anticipation that such goals can be realized if culturally appropriate action is taken.

Such an idea is carried forward in many of Tshibumba's paintings of Lumumba. Several scholars have noticed an intriguing commonality in the idiosyncrasies of Tshibumba's sense of perspective: there is a pronounced opposition between left and right sides of his pictures, with the former depicting troubling or violent elements, and the latter the anticipation of their resolution.[20] Lumumba often stands at the threshold between these sides, mediating them.

In a painting such as "Arrestation à Lodja" (fig. 45, p.77), for example, the left side of the painting shows two armed soldiers rushing toward a Peugeot sedan, while a third bends to open the door of the car, presumably to drag Lumumba from the vehicle. One of the running soldiers turns his head to peer menacingly at the viewer through dark sunglasses. Insignia on the soldiers' helmets mimic the flaming torch that would become the emblem of Mobutu's political party, making clear who is to blame for Lumumba's demise. Such reference and, indeed, painting Lumumba's image or even mentioning his name in public, were considered dangerously subversive in the mid-1970s (Jewsiewicki 1996:129).

FIG. 77.
A titleholder to King Kabongo wears a sculpted axe over his left shoulder to convey his status as well as his connections to Luba royalty. Such emblems are divine replicas of the weapons and tools that Luba culture heroes wielded in their struggles to found a new social order. Photo: Mary Nooter Roberts, Shaba Region, Democratic Republic of Congo, 1989.

Lumumba stands facing the viewer in such a way that he obscures most of the car, which surreally disappears behind him. His arms hang passively at his sides, his eyes are slightly downcast, and the highlights on his brow form a well-defined cross. Jewsiewicki (1996:136) convincingly asserts that these highlights reproduce ones caused by flashbulbs in a famous photograph of Lumumba. While this may have been the origin of the motif, the shape easily lends itself to interpretation as a cross, especially in Tshibumba's painting "La mort historique de Lumumba" (fig. 67, p.92), in which Lumumba's corpse lies on the ground after his assassination, his side pierced like Christ's. The cross on Lumumba's forehead echoes the three crosses of Calvary depicted in the right-hand portion of the picture.[21]

In his dejection after his arrest by Mobutu's soldiers (fig. 45, p.77), Lumumba seems to anticipate his imminent assassination. Narratives accompanying paintings of this theme produced by other Congolese popular artists explain that Lumumba could have escaped, but instead he chose to "face his destiny" and "freely agreed to die" (Jewsiewicki 1996:129, 133). Indeed, Jewsiewicki suggests that through the "Christ-like" Lumumba, urban-dwellers realize a convergence of saintly and political histories while "open[ing] to every person the possibility to join (s'inscrire) the process" (ibid.:119, 129).

The right side of "Arrestation à Lodja" is occupied by Lumumba's young son wearing what appears to be a school uniform. The child's eyes are closed in sadness or prayer. He reaches up as if seeking to be comforted, but Lumumba cannot take his son's hand, for he has given himself up to the great sacrifice of his "passion." Through reference to Jesus, viewers are led to anticipate that Lumumba's message *will* prevail, the chains of their oppression *will* be broken, and their dignity *will* someday be redeemed.

When a Luba chief or king takes office, he inherits royal metal emblems that recall the "forging of a king" ritual transforming an ordinary mortal into a semi-divine being who incarnates the culture heroes themselves. Photo: Mary Nooter Roberts, Shaba Region, Democratic Republic of Congo, 1989.

FIG. 79. (BELOW)
A Luba titleholder displays sacred insignia, worn on his person as he travels by foot to a neighboring village. A knife handle sculpted with Janus heads refers to the culture hero's dualistic nature, and reinforces a titleholder's role as mediator between yesterday's heroes and tomorrow's leaders. Photo: Mary Nooter Roberts, Shaba Region, Democratic Republic of Congo, 1988.

The Hero's Body as Locus of Memory

It is not only within the hero's body that the tensions of longing and the paradoxes of anticipation are articulated, but also within the bodies of various social actors who incarnate the spirits of Luba culture heroes. There are three contexts in which Luba officeholders perform memories of the culture heroes: royal investiture rites when every chief or king is imbued with the spirit of Kalala Ilunga; Mbudye initiation rites, which guide the novice from a state of ignorance associated with Nkongolo, to a state of divine enlightenment connected with Mbidi Kiluwe; and divination rites when diviners incarnate the spirit of the first diviner, Mijibu wa Kalenga, who assisted Kalala to overcome the cruelty of Nkongolo using devices Mbidi left with him in anticipation of just such challenges. The following will briefly recount these forms of Luba heroic embodiment.

When a Luba king or chief undergoes his investiture into office, he is said to incarnate the spirit of the first Luba king, Kalala Ilunga. In the past, successors to the throne underwent a rite called "the beating of the anvils," in which the candidate was seated upon a stool and made to hold a double-ended, iron-tipped spear and a ceremonial axe as the emblems of the original culture hero, while a dignitary symbolically beat the candidate's knees with a pillar anvil (also used as a blacksmith's hammer) to reenact the "forging of a king." Just as a blacksmith transforms raw metal into useful weapons and tools, so the dignitaries transform an ordinary man into a divine ruler with supernatural abilities (Dewey and Childs 1996) (fig. 78). And just as Mbidi Kiluwe and Kalala Ilunga introduced advanced iron-working technologies that would contribute to the kingdom's ascent to power, so every king incarnates these origins. Yet, the point of such rituals is not to recreate the past *as past,* but to gather up the past and bring it into the present. Gripping the emblems inherited directly from the culture hero, the new king is transformed through embodiment of the avatar of change itself (fig. 80).

Heroic embodiment also structures the initiation of all Luba officials into the Mbudye society responsible for protecting and transmitting Luba history and royal precepts. In this context, embodiment is connected with the acquisition of knowledge, and identification with the culture heroes brings intellectual and spiritual enlightenment. When novices are still in the first two stages of initiation, they are associated with the antihero Nkongolo, and their skin is covered in charcoal to signify the inchoate nature of their uninitiated state. As novices ascend the initiation ladder, they become progressively whitened with chalk to signify their gradual enlightenment through and into the secrets of Luba royalty (fig. 82). When an initiate reaches the two highest levels of Mbudye, s/he undergoes spirit possession, during which s/he "becomes" a particular spirit but also incarnates the spirit of Mbidi Kiluwe in a totalizing way (M. Roberts 1996). The term for spirit possession, *kutentama,* is the same word used to describe the rising of a new moon so closely connected with the dichotomous hero Mbidi, who is lunar like the Roman god Janus. At this stage, the initiate is graced by the white clairvoyance of "the rising of a new moon" (Roberts 1985) through a process called "breaking through the sky" (Nooter 1991:106-110). Only then is the initiate ready to absorb the secrets revealed in the complex landscape of memory that is the lukasa board.

FIG. 80.
At every royal ceremony and especially during investiture rites, Luba chiefs and their dignitaries enact episodes of the Luba epic. Here, Twite, a High-ranking officeholder, dances before King Kabongo wielding a ceremonial axe in remembrance of the culture hero Kalala Ilunga.
Photo: Mary Nooter Roberts, Shaba Region, Democratic Republic of Congo, 1989.

FIG. 81. (BELOW)
Half Figure. Pare peoples, Tanzania. 19th century. Clay, pigment, beads. H. 6 in. The Stanley Collection of The University of Iowa Museum of Art. Culture heroes in eastern and central Africa are frequently characterized as dichotomous beings, as is the Luba hero, Mbidi Kiluwe. This Pare half-figure evokes the paradox of such dialectic, for in lacking limbs, it years for completion.

During Mbudye rituals and important ceremonies of state, Mbudye members enter possession states in order to perform didactic dances that enact specific episodes from the Luba epic. For example, one dance is a dramatic staging of Nkongolo's wicked invitation to his sister's son, Kalala Ilunga, to dance upon a woven mat covering a pit trap filled with upright spears. Following Mbidi Kiluwe's anticipation of such duplicitousness, the first Luba spirit medium, Mijibu wa Kalenga, instructs Kalala to listen closely to the drummer who safely guides his footsteps through coded tonal messages. Mbudye members who perform this dance wield a spear as they tumble and twirl around the arena as did/does Kalala (fig. 84). This pivotal episode, and many others like it, form the basis of theatrical and highly acrobatic dances that Mbudye still offer in the rural Luba region, as choreographic embodiments of the culture heroes themselves.

The dance brings attention to a third context of embodied heroism in Luba practice: diviners' roles in shaping histories. All Luba spirit mediums, male and female, past and present, consider themselves to be incarnations of Mijibu wa Kalenga.[22] Whenever a Luba medium holds a consultation these days, s/he must first enter into a state of spirit possession, during which s/he is said to incarnate both a particular regional spirit, as well as the spirit of Mijibu wa Kalenga. Throughout the course of Luba precolonial, colonial, and postcolonial political history, Bilumbu have served as counselors, advisors, and protectors of kings and chiefs. All important decisions affecting the state are brought before them, and Bilumbu continue to address the needs of individuals, families, factions, and village groupings. Through spirit possession diviners conflate past and present in an ever-evolving drama of social accommodation as they seek a perfected future. It is through use of sacred objects and spirit-possession practices that diviners incarnate Mijibu wa Kalenga to affect these protective and prophetic roles (figs. 83, 87).[23]

The prominence of Kalala Ilunga and his close relationship to Mijibu wa Kalenga is such that the two constitute a single semantic unit. The entire Luba political structure is posited on the interdependence of the two institutions of kingship and divination, as is repeatedly reenacted through the divination rituals of everyday life. Mijibu's name has come to stand for the institution of Bulumbu as a whole, and is inseparable from the concept of kingship. For, each time that a diviner goes into a state of possession, he becomes Mijibu, just as during the sacred investiture rites, every king is Kalala Ilunga.

Conclusion: Surpassing Signifiers

For heartland Luba, the culture hero does not inhere in any object or container apart from particular people's own bodies. Social actors are not recipients or extensions of an originary royalty; rather, they *are* that royalty. Through the lexicon of spirit possession, Luba rulers, diviners, and Mbudye members attain political legitimacy and personal "authenticity" by means of and within their own bodies. And following the dichotomous model of Mbidi Kiluwe, they can alternate between the realities of life in the present, and more ancient realities that are always present but can either recede into the dark secrecy of suspended potentiality, or project forward to a future that will have been. In so doing, they surpass the role of the signifier.

No simple signifier remains discrete. Luba sculptures may not portray culture heroes, but most depict female beings—a gendering which may seem to contradict the previous assertion. Yet Luba heroes transcend gender. Luba feel that the female body is the most effective container for spiritual power, and while some female images adorning staffs, stools, and spears are said to depict a chief's or king's mother, wife, or sister, more usually the reference is to women's capacity to receive and hold the intense spirits of kings (figs. 85, 86). Luba often refer to royalty as a woman: "the king is a woman," they say, but Mijibu wa Kalenga is "a woman" too, and even the Mbudye association is "a woman" (see Nooter 1991: Ch.5; idem 1999b). These commonly heard remarks are not contradictory, but reflect a deliberate ambiguation of gender that can accommodate the

paradoxical duality of power as Luba understand it.[24] Luba perceive power to be both male and female at once, then, and the overt, outwardly directed leadership qualities of men are counterbalanced by the covert, mysterious, and secretive powers of women. This additional dualism further reinforces the divided nature of heroes, who embody both male and female elements, and whose memories invoke and transcend the "double-coding" of gender.[25]

It is a hero's "double-coding" and the vulnerability of the hero's nomadic nature that give hagiography its compelling force to live a past in the present. Hagiography is embodied narrative: it is biography that becomes autobiographical for the reader, as the story of an Other that is the story of one's Self. A life history with "exhortative force" becomes lodged in the reader's affective body. The contexts in which Luba kings, spirit mediums, and Mbudye members become culture heroes are always moments of the most dramatic upheaval—loss of a great leader, an ordinary man's ascent to extraordinary kingship, an uninitiated person's acquisition of empowering esoteric knowledge, a patient's quest for healing and redemption through divination. Likewise, in contexts of contemporary popular painting, culture heroes are portrayed at moments of civil strife, resistance, or urban disenfranchisement. Lumumba looms in the paintings as an omen of transformation and hope.

If longing is the continual search and "yearning desire" for immortality (Stewart 1993:ix-x), culture heroes for Luba and other Bantu-speaking peoples invoke collective nostalgia in preparing people to overcome traumatic circumstances. The anticipation implicit to their divided nature is the knowledge of transformative, difficult, and permanent metamorphosis that lies in the realm of the future-perfect. The familiar notion that culture heroes represent an ideal, mythical past is in precise opposition to the Congolese cases we have considered, in which Janus-like culture heroes embody becoming. As the point "where narrative begins/ends, both engendering and transcending the relation between materiality and meaning" (ibid.:x), culture heroes herald transition and transformation as history envisions and invents itself anew.

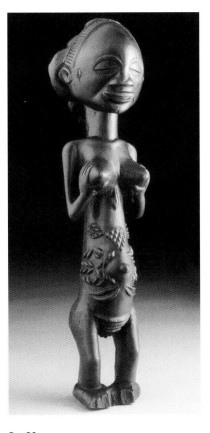

Fig. 87.
Bowl Figure. Luba peoples, Democratic Republic of Congo. 19th century. Wood. H. 11 in. The Stanley Collection of The University of Iowa Museum of Art. Luba spokespersons often identified wooden sculptures of a women holding a bowl as the wife of a diviner's possessing spirit, or as Mijibu wa Kalenga, the first Luba diviner who is a culture hero in his own right. Present-day Luba diviners still own figures like this one, that house the diviner-hero's spirit.

Fig. 85.
Detail of Ceremonial Spear shown in fig. 74. Luba emblems are double-coded, just like the heroes that they commemorate. This spear's owner gripped the past while anticipating the future, and though such an individual was most probably a man, he knew that the wellspring of his power lay in the hands of royal women.

Fig. 86.
Female Figure. Luba peoples, Shaba Region, Democratic Republic of Congo. 19th century. Wood. H. 14 in. The Stanley Collection of The University of Iowa Museum of Art. Like Christian saints, Luba culture heroes often transcend gender. Luba emblems are almost always fashioned as female figures, for although they represent male culture heroes' exploits and contributions, they protect the spirits of these heroes through the most effective receptacle of spiritual embodiment—a woman's body.

1. *Ukumbusho* is "an abstract noun formed from a causative verb," derived from *kukumbuka* in Swahili—"to remember" (Fabian 1996:195).

2. Both authors conducted predoctoral research in Shaba Region of Zaire, after 1997 known as Katanga Province, Democratic Republic of the Congo (DRC). The "ethnographic present" used in this text refers to the Zairian period of Congolese history. Mary's two years of fieldwork among heartland Luba (1987-1989) and year of archival research in Belgium were funded by an American Association of University Women Dissertation Fellowship, a Wenner-Gren Foundation for Anthropological Research Grant-in-Aid, a Belgian-American Educational Foundation Fellowship, a Columbia University Wittkower Fellowship, and a Smithsonian Institution Pre-Doctoral Fellowship. Allen's forty-five months among lakeside Tabwa (1974-1977) and subsequent archival research were funded by the U.S. National Institute of Mental Health, the Committee on African Studies and the Edson-Keith Fund of the University of Chicago, Sigma Xi the Scientific Research Society, an National Endowment for the Humanities Summer Stipend and exhibition implementation grant at the University of Michigan Museum of Art, Mellon Foundation Faculty Development Grants via Albion College, The Museum for African Art of New York City, and the Project for Advanced Study of Art and Life in Africa at the University of Iowa. Thanks to Barbara Thompson for ethnographic insight. For our children, Sid, Seth, and Avery.

3. For a summary of precolonial political history in the Luba region, see Vansina 1966, Reefe 1981, Roberts 1985 and 1989, and Roberts and Roberts 1996. Recent history prior to the death of Mobutu in 1997 is reviewed in Young 1994.

4. In their writing on the cultural construction of Africa, Bogumil Jewsiewicki and V. Y. Mudimbe critique the artificial distinctions that outsiders have created among precolonial, colonial, and post-colonial periods of the Congo (1993:3). As they argue, such socio-political transitions are more fluidly interwoven than such categories suggest. For discussion of the bridging from precolonial to postcolonial periods in African arts, see Vogel 1991. For consideration of African art historical applications of the term "invented traditions" as developed by Hobsbawm and Ranger (1983), and for discussion of the flexibility and fluidity implicit to "tradition," see Jewsiewiski 1990, and Vogel 1990:32.

5. See Fabian 1998: chapter two, for cogent discussion of "genres in popular culture." Bogumil Jewsiewicki discusses in this volume ways that Congolese sought to understand the arbitrary tyrannies of Mobutu's rule, and the seductions of capitalism in the cities of the Congolese Copperbelt.

6. The term "culture hero" is problematic and merits reconsideration, or, perhaps extension. Is this word used in Western contexts? Or is it reserved for non-Western cultures for whom the factual historicity of such persons is doubted by outsiders, so that the characters are considered mythical? What would or would not emerge if one were to call Jesus Christ or the Prophet Muhammad a "culture hero"?

7. We are currently engaged in research in urban Senegal on popular devotional arts associated with the Mouride Sufi movement and its founding saint *(wali Allah,* or "friend of God"), Cheikh Amadou Bamba (d.1927). "'Passport to Paradise': Senegalese Sufi Arts on the Move" will result as a book and exhibition at UCLA's Fowler Museum of Cultural History in 2001. This project will be followed by a comparison of Mouride "visual piety" with that of followers of Sai Baba of Shirdi (d.1918), a Hindu/Muslim saint of India, as well as saints of Christianity and other world religions.

8. Memory literature from a number of disciplines in the humanities and social sciences is reviewed in Roberts and Roberts 1996.

9. Also see Jewsiewicki 1988 for discussion of collective memory and the *"passé présent"* in popular Congolese historical discourse.

10. For further reading on emplacement and the philosophy of place, see E. Casey 1987, 1993, and 1997.

11. Other scholars have brought attention to this attribute of popular painting. For example, Crawford Young writes that "in the case of *colonie belge,* the subliminal message is certain: the artist through the medium of history is painting the present" (1992:131). Johannes Fabian entitles his book, *Remembering the Present* (1996) to capture the paradox of temporal simultaneity, and in *Moments of Freedom* (1998), he explains how in popular arts, such a "way with time" is a "weapon of the weak."

12. An important model for such representation is European imaging of the Virgin Mary in the Middle Ages, through which Mary reflects sadness in her tender gaze upon the infant Jesus whom she holds in her arms, "anticipating the sorrows to come" in Christ's Passion (Belting 1994:285). Our thinking concerning the "future perfect" dimension of Luba culture heroes and Tshibumba's paintings has been influenced by Hans Belting's magnificent study, *Likeness and Presence* (1994).

13. The present tense here indicates that precolonial ideas inform current experience, as will be explained.

14. For primary documents and discussions of the Luba epic, see Heusch 1982a, Mudimbe 1991, and Reefe 1981.

15. The same names are sometimes pronounced and spelled differently according to transcription, dialects, and local languages: Lunda is also Aruund or Ruwund; Chibinda Ilunga can be Cibind Yirung; and Lueji is also Ruwej (see Palmeirim 1998:21).

16. The West's preoccupation with African sculpture, and especially that which depicts human or spirit beings, over other forms of African expressive culture is a cultural bias that rarely reflects African aesthetics and systems of value; see Nooter 1992:84 and passim.

17. The phrase "dichotomous beings" is from Needham 1980:29. On these half-beings in central Africa, see Roberts 1986b, 1986c. See Heusch 1982b:252-255, 269 for examples among Bantu-speaking peoples elsewhere in Africa.

18. Our most recent consideration of threshold effects is in our book, *A Sense of Wonder* (Roberts and Roberts 1997), through two brief essays on the fantastic and the sublime in African art.

19. Our hanging crescent horseshoes above doorways still reflects ancient Roman practice, in recognition of the protection afforded thresholds by the lunar god Janus (Schilling 1960:174).

20. See Biaya 1992:161-163, Dupré 1992:148, and Jewsiewicki 1996:132-134.

21. The ways that contemporary Christians (and presumably missionaries) discern hidden symbols in portraits of Jesus are discussed by David Morgan (1998:128-129), who notes that whereas Warner Sallman denied he had consciously painted a cross into his well-known popular painting, "Head of Christ" in 1940, he pointed it out in the "chalk talks" he offered during which he would sketch the same picture.

22. "Bilumbu" is the plural proper name for such spirit mediums, "kilumbu" is the singular, and "Bulumbu" is the entire realm of divination. Another name for spirit mediums in current usage is "Bwana Vidye," which serves as a generic honorific title. Bulumbu is also found among some neighboring groups such as Tabwa (Roberts 1989).

23. Even with the most traumatic changes wrought by colonialism, capitalism, Catholicism, and postcolonial political tyranny, Bulumbu persists as an active institution of healing, litigation, and decision-making. It is a profession that has fluidly adapted to change through continuous updating of its own ideological premises, such as the invention of new spirits and new techniques, while always holding fast to the formative roots of the institution. For a detailed analysis of Luba divination practices, see Mary Roberts' forthcoming article entitled "Proofs and Promises: Setting Meaning Before the Eyes" (M. Roberts 1999a).

24. "Ambiguate" appears to be our neologism, for although "disambiguate" is a word in English, the former is not, presumably because the positivist philosophy undergirding English always leads away from ambiguity, rather than toward it. Luba dualistic gendering of power is expressed by the fact that until quite recently, when a king died, his spirit was incarnated by a woman named Mwadi, whose role was to perpetuate the "kingdom of the dead" and preserve the king's memory for posterity (see M. Roberts 1999). It appears that the role of Mwadi ceased with the death of the last woman of this title in the 1980s. On notions of power among peoples of southern DRC, see Fabian 1990.

25. See Wyschograd (1990:xxiii-iv) for a related discussion of the double-coding of saints; and Morgan (1998: Ch.3), on the blurred gender of Jesus.

Bibliography

General works

Agamben, Giorgio
1996 *L'homme sans contenu*. Paris.

Badi-Banga ne-Mwine
1977 *Contribution à l'étude historique de l'art plastique zaïrois moderne*. Kinshasa.

Bastin, Marie-Louise
1978 *Statuettes tshokwe du héros civilisateur 'Tshibinda Ilunga'*. Arnouville.

Belting, Hans
1994 *Likeness and Presence: A History of the Image Before the Era of Art*. Chicago.

Blok, Anton
1991 "Reflections on 'Making History.'" *In Other Histories*. K. Hastrup (ed.). London.

Casey, Edward
1987 *Remembering: A Phenomenological Study*. Bloomington.

1993 *Getting back into Place: Toward a Renewed Understanding of the Place-World*. Bloomington and Indianapolis.

1997 *The Fate of Place: A Philosophical History*. Berkeley, Los Angeles, London.

Childs, S. Terry, and Pierre de Maret
1996 "Re/Constructing Luba Pasts." In *Memory: Luba Art and the Making of History*. Mary Nooter Roberts and Allen F. Roberts (eds.) New York and Munich.

Colas Musa
1992 "*Récit de la mort de Bwana François*." In *Art pictural zaïrois*, B. Jewsiewicki (ed.). Sillery, (Québec.)

Cornelis, Sabine
1998 "Romain-Desfossés." *Biographie belge d'outre-mer*. Brussel.

Cornet, Joseph-Aurélien
1992 *Peintres de Lubumbashi (Bela, Pili-Pili, Mwenze)*. Paris.

Cornet, Joseph-Aurélien, Rémi De Cnodder, Wim Toebosch
1989 *60 ans de peinture au Zaïre*. Brussels.

Deleuze, Gilles
1992 "Mediator." In *Incorporations*, J. Crary and S. Kwinter (eds.). New York.

Dewey, William and S. Terry Childs
1996 "Forging Memory." In *Memory: Luba Art and the Making of History*. New York and Munich.

Dibwe dia Mwembu
1985 "*Un chef songye face au pouvoir colonial. Cas du chef Lumpungu (1892-1919).*" *Cahiers de Tunisie*, 33 (133-134): 49-70.

Fabian, Johannes
1983 *Time and the Other*. New York.

1986 *Language and Colonial Power: The Appropriation of Swahili in the Former Belgian Congo, 1880-1938*. Cambridge.

1990 *Power and Performance: Ethnographic Explorations Through Proverbial Wisdom and Theater in Shaba, Zaire*. Madison.

1996 *Remembering the Present: Painting and Popular History in Zaire*. Berkeley, Los Angeles, London.

1998 *Moments of Freedom: Anthropology and Popular Culture*. Charlottesville and London.

Flexner, Stuart (ed.)
1987 *The Random House Dictionary of the English Language*, 2nd ed. New York.

Freedberg, David
1989 *The Power of Images*. Chicago.

Geeraerts, Jeff
1995 *Black Venus*. Arles and Bruxelles.

Glissant, Edouard
1993 *Tout-Monde*. Paris.

Gondola, Didier
1998 "Dream and Drama: The Search for Elegance among Congolese Youth." *African Studies Review*, 41(3): forthcoming november 1998.

Grimal, Pierre
1945 "*Le dieu Janus et les origines de Rome*," *Lettres d'Humanité* 4:15-121.

Heusch, Luc de
1982a *The Drunken King, or, The Origin of the State*. Bloomington.

1982b *Rois nés d'un coeur de vache*. Paris.

1988 "*Le Vipère et la Cigogne: Notes sur le symbolisme tshokwe*." In *Art et Mythologie: Figures Tshokwe*. Paris.

1991 "The King Comes from Elsewhere." In *Body and Space: Symbolic Models of Unity and Division in African Cosmology and Experience*. A. Jacobson-Widding (ed.). *Uppsala Studies in Cultural Anthropology*, vol. 16. Stockholm.

Hobsbawm, Eric and Terence Ranger (eds.)
1983 *The Invention of Tradition*. London.

Jewsiewicki, Bogumil
1987 "*La mort de Bwana François à Elisabethville: la mémoire, l'imaginaire et la connaissance du passé*." *Annales Aequatoria* 8: 405-413.

1991a "*La mémoire*," *Les Afriques politiques*. Chistian Coulon and Denis Martin, (eds.). Paris.

1991b "Painting in Zaire: From the Invention of the West to the Representation of Social Self." In *Africa Explores:20th Century African Art*. Susan Vogel (ed.), assisted by Ima Ebong. New York and Munich

1995 *Chéri Samba. The Hybridity of Art*. Montreal.

Jewsiewicki, Bogumil, ed.
1989 *Art and Politics in Black Africa*. Ottawa.

1992 *Art pictural zaïrois*. Sillery (Québec).

Jewsiewicki, Bogumil and V.Y. Mudimbe
1993 "Africans' History and Contemporary History of Africa." *History and Theory: Studies in the Philosophy of History* 32(4): 1-11.

Jordán, Manuel
1993 "*Le masque comme processus ironique: Les makishi du nord-ouest de la Zambie.*" *Anthropologie et Sociétés* 17(3):41-46.

Jordán, Manuel (ed.)
1998 *Chokwe! Art and Initiation Among Chokwe and Related Peoples*. Munich and Birmingham.

Jules-Rosette, Bennetta
1992 "What is 'Popular?' The Relationship Between Zairian Popular and Tourist Paintings." In *Art pictural zaïrois*. B. Jewsiewicki (ed.). Sillery (Québec).

Kabuya-Lumuna Sando
1995 *La conquête des libertés en Afrique*, Kinshasa.

Kalulambi Pongo, Martin
1997 *Être Luba au Xxe siècle. Ethnicité et identité chrétienne au Congo démocratique* (Zaïre). Paris.

Kayamba Badye
1995-1996 "*Conflits entho-politiques et paix civile au Katanga.*" *Likundoli: Archives et documents* 16: 30-56.

Lundula Passou
1994 *Lettre ouverte à Monseigneur Monsengw.* Lubumbashi.

Morgan, David
1998 *Visual Piety: A History and Theory of Popular Religious Images*. Berkeley.

Mudimbe, V. Y.
1988 *The Invention of Africa*. Bloomington.

1991 *Parables and Fables: Exegesis, Textuality, and Politics in Central Africa*. Madison.

1996 "The Idea of 'Luba.'" In *Memory: Luba Art and the Making of History*. New York and Munich.

Needham, Rodney
1980 *Reconnaissances.* Buffalo.

Nooter, Mary H.
1991 "Luba Art and Polity: Creating Power in a Central African Kingdom." Unpublished Ph.D. dissertation, Columbia University.

1992 "Fragments of Forsaken Glory: Luba Royal Culture Invented and Represented (1883-1992)." In *Kings of Africa: Art and Authority in Central Africa*. Maastricht.

Nora, Pierre
1984 *Les lieux des mémoire*, vol. 1., *La République*. Paris.

1989 "Between Memory and History." In *Memory and Countermemory.* N. Davis and R. Starn (eds.). *Representations* 26:7-25.

1998 *Realms of Memory: The Construction of the French Past*. American ed. of *Lieux de mémoire*. New York.

Nzunguba Ibio, Jean-Pierre
1994 "*Peintres, peintures et culture populaire à Bunia (Zaïre): essai d'analyse socio-historique.*" Ph.D. dissertation, Université Laval, Québec.

Palmeirim, Manuela
1998 "The King's Crowns: Hierarchy in the Making Among the Aruwund (Lunda)." In *Chokwe: Art and Initiation Among Chokwe and Related Peoples*. M. Jordán (ed.). Munich and Birmingham.

Reefe, Thomas Q.
1981 *The Rainbow and the Kings: A History of the Luba Empire to 1891*. Berkeley.

Roberts, Allen F.
1980 "Heroic Beasts, Beastly Heroes: Principles of Cosmology and Chiefship Among the Lakeside BaTabwa of Zaire." Unpublished Ph.D. dissertation, The University of Chicago.

1985 "Social and Historical Contexts of Tabwa Art." In *The Rising of a New Moon: A Century of Tabwa Art*. Allen F. Roberts and Evan Maurer (eds.). Seattle.

1986a "The Comeuppance of ' Mr. Snake' and Other Tales of Survival from Contemporary Rural Zaire." In *The Crisis in Zaire: Myths and Realities*, Nzongola-Ntalaj (ed.). Trenton.

1986b "Duality in Tabwa Art." *African Arts* l9 (4): 26-35, 86-88.

1986c "*Les arts du corps chez les Tabwa.*" *Arts d'Afriquen noire* 59:l5-20.

1989 "History, Ethnicity and Change in the 'Christian Kingdom' of Southeastern Zaire." In *The Creation of Tribalism in South and Central Africa: Studies in the Political Economy of Ideology*. L. Val, (ed.). Berkeley.

1991 "Where the King is Coming From." In *Body and Space: Symbolic Models of Unity and Division in African Cosmology and Experience*. A. Jacobson-Widding (ed.). *Uppsala Studies in Cultural Anthropology* 16:249-269.

1992. "Neither Here Nor There/Weder Hier Noch Dort." In *Threshold States/Sprach-Schwellen*, H. Breder (ed.). Münster.

1993 "Insight, or, NOT Seeing is Believing." In *SECRECY: African Art that Conceals and Reveals*, M. Nooter (ed.).New York.

1996 "Peripheral Visions." In *Memory: Luba Art and the Making of History*. M. Nooter Roberts and A. Roberts (eds.). Munich and New York.

Roberts, Mary Nooter
1999a "Proofs and Promises: Setting Meaning Before the Eye." In *Art and Divination*. John Pemberton III (ed.). Washington, D.C.

1999b "The King is a Woman: Gender and Authority in Central African Art." In *Nature, Belief, and Ritual: Art of Sub-Saharan Africa at the Dallas Museum of Art*. Dallas.

1996 "Luba Memory Theater." In *Memory: Luba Art and the Making of History*. M. Nooter Roberts and A. Roberts (eds.). Munich and New York.

Roberts, Mary Nooter and Allen Roberts. (eds)
1996 *Memory: Luba Art and the Making of History*. New York and Munich.

1997 *A Sense of Wonder: African Art from the Faletti Family Collection*. Seattle and Phoenix.

Roy, Christopher (ed.)
1992 *Art and Life in Africa: Selections from the Stanley Collection, Exhibitions of 1985 and 1992*. Seattle and Iowa City.

Sartre, Jean-Paul
1956 *Being and Nothingness*. New York.

Schilling, M. Robert
1960 "*Janus, le dieu introducteur, le dieu de passage.*" *Mélanges d'Archéologie et d'Histoire, École Française de Rome* 72: 89-131.

Shearer, Alistair
1993 *The Hindu Vision: Forms of the Formless*. London.

Stewart, Susan
1993 *On Longing: Narratives of the Miniature, the Gigantic, the Souvenir, the Collection*. Durham and London.

Theuws, T.
1968 "*Le Styx ambigü.*" *Bulletin du Centre d'étude des problèmes sociaux indigènes* 81: 5-33.

Toebosch, Wim
1992 "*L'école d'Elisabethville.*" In *MRAC, La naissance de la peinture contempo- raine en Afrique centrale 1930-1970*. Tervuren.

Turner, Victor
1955 "A Lunda Love Story and Its Consequences." *Rhodes-Livingstone Journal* 19: 1-26.

Vansina, Jan
1966 *Kingdoms of the Savanna*. Madison.

Vellut, Jean-Luc
1992 "Une exécution publique à Elisabethville (20 septembre 1922). Notes sur la pratique de la peine capitale dans l'histoire coloniale du Congo." In *Art pictural zaïrois*. B. Jewsiewicki (ed.). Sillery (Québec).

Verhulpen, Edmund
1936 *Baluba et Balubaïsés du Katanga*. Antwerp.

Vincke, Édouard
1992 "*Un outil ethno- graphique: la peinture populaire contemporaine au Zaïre.*" In *Art pictural zaïrois*. B. Jewsiewicki (ed.). Sillery (Québec).

Vogel, Susan (ed.), asst. Ima Ebong
1991 *Africa Explores: 20th Century African Art*. New York and Munich.

Wyschograd, Edith
1990 *Saints and Postmodernism: Revisioning Moral Philosophy*. Chicago.

Yates, Frances
1966 *The Art of Memory*. Chicago.

Young, Crawford
1992 "Painting the Burden of the Past: History as Tragedy." In *Art pictural zaïrois*. B. Jewsiewicki (ed.). Sillery (Québec).

1994 "Zaire: The Shattered Illusion of the Integral State." *Journal of Modern African Studies* 32(2): 247-263.

Works on Patrice Lumumba

Anonymous
1997 "Extraits du Journal d'un magistrat colonial (juillet-septembre 1959)." In Patrice Lumumba entre dieu et diable. Un héros africain dans ses images. Pierre Halen and János Riesz (eds.). Paris.

Bakajika Banjikila
1975 "Le rôle de l'évolué congolais dans l'accession de son pays à l'indépendance nationale." In Elites et devenir de la société zaïroise Lubumbashi. Actes des troisièmes journées d'histoire du Zaïre. CERDAC, 14 - 17 mai 1975. Lubumbashi.

Brassine, Jacques and Jean Kestergat
1991 Qui a tué Patrice Lumumba. Paris.

Césaire, Aimé
1973 [1967] Une Saison au Congo. Paris.

Chomé, Jules
1961 M. Lumumba et le communisme. Brussels.

Clément, Pierre
1960 "Patrice Lumumba (Stanleyville 1952–1953)." Présence Africaine 40: 57–78.

Coquery-Vidrovitch, Catherine, Alain Forest and Herbert Weiss, eds.
1987 Rébellions-Révolution au Zaïre 1963-1965. Paris.

Djungu-Simba, Charles K.
1997 "La Figure de Patrice Lumumba dans les lettres du Congo-Zaïre: quelques observations." In Patrice Lumumba entre dieu et diable. Un héros africain dans ses images. Pierre Halen, and János Riesz (eds.). Paris.

Devos, Pierre
1961 Vie et mort de Lumumba. Paris.

Fanon, Frantz
1967 " Lumumba's Death: Could We Do Otherwise? " In Toward the African Revolution., New York.

Gilbert, O. P.
1947 L'Empire du silence. Congo 1946. Brussels.

Halen, Pierre, and Riesz, János (eds.)
1997 Patrice Lumumba entre dieu et diable. Un héros africain dans ses images. Paris.

Heinz, G., and Donnay, H.
1969 [1966] Lumumba. The Last Fifty Days. New York.

Heusch, Luc de
1962 "Plidoyer à la mémoire de Patrice Lumumba." Synthèse 189: 25-32.

Houart, Pierre
1960 Pénétration communiste au Congo. Brussels.

Houyoux, Serge
1993 Quand Césaire écrit, Lumumba parle. Paris.

Hoyet, Marie-Josée
1997 "Quelques images de Patrice Lumumba dans la littérature du monde noir d'expression française." In Patrice Lumumba entre dieu et diable. Un héros africain dans ses images. Pierre Halen and János Riesz (eds.). Paris.

Jewsiewicki, Bogumil
1996 "Corps interdits. La représentation christique de Lumumba comme redempteur du peuple zaïrois." Cahiers d'études africaines 141-142: 113-142.

Kalb, Madeleine
1982 The Congo Cables. The Cold War in Africa from Eisenhower to Kennedy. New York.

Kapita, Mulopo
1992 P. Lumumba. Justice pour le héros. Paris.

Kashamura, Anicet
1966 De Lumumba aux colonels. Paris.

Kanza, Thomas
1978 The Rise and Fall of P. Lumumba. Conflict in the Congo. London.

Kestergat, Jean
1986 Du Congo de Lumumba au Zaïre de Mobutu. Brussels.

Legum, Colin.
1966 "The Life and Death of Patrice Lumumba." Foreword in Congo, My Country. P. Lumumba. New York.

Lemarchand, René.
1964 Political Awakening in the Belgian Congo. Berkeley & Los Angeles.

Lopez Alvares, L.
1964 Lumumba ou l'Afrique frustrée. Paris.

Lory, G.
1989 "La jeunesse de Lumumba." Jeune Afrique Plus 1: 84-91.

Lumumba, Patrice
1954 "Un explorateur incomparable." In La Voix du Congolais, 100.

1966 [1962] Congo, My Country. New York. Original ver., Congo, terre d'avenir, est-il menacé? Brussels, 1961.

1972 "Weep, o Beloved Black Brother." In Lumumba Speaks. Jean Van Lierde (ed.). Little. Originally "Pleure, o Noir frère bien-aimé." In Indépendance. September, 1959.

Makolo Muswaswa, Bertin
1997 "Quelques chansons populaires de l'État autonome du Sud Kasai." In Patrice Lumumba entre dieu et diable. Un héros africain dans ses images. Pierre Halen and János Riesz (eds.). Paris.

Manya K'Omalowete a Djonga
1985 Patrice Lumumba, le Sankuru et l'Afrique. Lutry (Genève).

Masuy, Christine
1997 "Du portrait au personnage. La diabolisation symbolique de Patrice Lumumba dans La Libre Belgique." In Patrice Lumumba entre dieu et diable. Un héros africain dans ses images. Pierre Halen and János Riesz (eds.). Paris.

Mbuyamba Kankolongo, Alphonse
1997 "Quelques témoignages sur Lumumba." In Patrice Lumumba entre dieu et diable. Un héros africain dans ses images. Pierre Halen and János Riesz (eds.). Paris.

McKown, Robin
1969 Lumumba. A Biography. Garden City.

Merriam, Alan
1961 Congo. Background of Conflict. Evanston.

Michel, Stéphane
1961 Uhuru Lumumba, Paris.

Musambachime Mwelwa C.
1987 "The Changing Political Personality of an African Politician: the Case of Patrice Lumumba, 1956-1961." Genève-Afrique 25(2): 61-78.

Mutamba Makombo, Jean-Marie
1993 "Patrice Lumumba correspondant de presse (1948-1956)." Cahiers africains no 3.

Omasombo Tshonda, Jean
1993 "Une tribu remémore sa crise: les Atetela." In Le Zaïre à l'épreuve de l'histoire immédiate. Hommage à Benoît Verhaegen. Jean Omasombo Tshonda (ed.). Paris.

Omasombo Tshonda, Jean and Benoît Verhaegen
1998 "Patrice Lumumba. Jeunesse et apprentissage politique, 1925-1956." Cahiers africains, no 33-34.

Peck, Raoul, director
1992 Lumumba: Death of a Prophet. Film originally in French, Lumumba: la mort du prophète.

Porra, Véronique
1997 "L'Afrique du Che. Du mythe de Lumumba à la réalité de la guerilla." In Patrice Lumumba entre dieu et diable. Un héros africain dans ses images. Pierre Halen and János Riesz (eds.). Paris.

Ricard, Alain
1997 "Patrice Lumumba, héros nigérian?" In Patrice Lumumba entre dieu et diable. Un héros africain dans ses images. Pierre Halen and János Riesz (eds.). Paris.

Rouch, Jean
1961 En cage avec Lumumba. Paris.

Rubango, Nyunda ya
1997 "Patrice Lumumba en son temps: un modéré?" In Patrice Lumumba entre dieu et diable. Un héros africain dans ses images. Pierre Halen and János Riesz (eds.). Paris.

Sartre, Jean-Paul
1963 "La pensée politique de Patrice Lumumba." In La pensée politique de Patrice Lumumba. Jean Van Lierde. Paris.

Simons, Edwine, Roupen Boghossian, Benoît Verhaegen
1995 "Stanleyville 1959. Le procès de Patrice Lumumba et les émeutes d'octobre." Cahiers africains, no. 17-18.

Tournaire Hélène and Robert Bouteaud
1963 Le livre noir du Congo. Congo, Katanga, Angola. Paris.

Turner, Thomas
1997 " Lumumba delivers the Congo from Slavery." "Patrice Lumumba in the minds of the Tetela." In Patrice Lumumba entre dieu et diable. Un héros africain dans ses images. Pierre Halen and János Riesz (eds.). Paris.

Valodine, L.
1961 Patrice Lumumba, champion de la liberté africaine. Moscow.

Van Lierde, Jean
1961 "Témoignage: Patrice Lumumba, leader et ami." Présence Africaine 36: 112–119.

1963 La pensée politique de Patrice Lumumba. Paris.

1988 Patrice Lumumba. La dimension d'un tribun. Charleroi.

Van Lierde, Jean, ed.
1972 Lumumba Speaks. Little. Original ver., La pensée politique de Patrice Lumumba. Paris, 1963.

Verhaegen, Benoît
1970 "Les associations congolaises à Léopoldville et dans le Bas-Congo de 1944 à 1958." In Études africaines du CRISP no. 112-113.

1977 "Patrice Emery Lumumba." In Les Africains. Paris.

1978 "Patrice Lumumba. Martyr d'une Afrique nouvelle." Jeune Afrique 891: 69–96.

1983 "L'association des évolués de Stanleyville et les débuts de P. Lumumba." In Les Cahiers du CEDAF, no 2.

1993 "Contribution à la bibliographie politique de Patrice Lumumba." Bulletin des séances de l'Académie Royale des Sciences d'Outre-Mer 39: 597–610.

Willame, Jean-Claude
1990 Patrice Lumumba. La crise congolaise revisitée. Paris.

Yoka Lye Mudaba
1992 "Gloire et honneur à un héros tragique." In P. Lumumba. Justice pour le héros. Mulopo Kapita. Paris. Original ver. in Le Soft de Finance (January 28, 1991).